FIVE

A Tale of Human Potential

———————

Bryant K. Smith

Five; A Tale of Human Potential
Copyright © 2009 by Bryant K. Smith

ISBN 978-1-4700676-6-3

Cover Design by: Bryant K. Smith
Edited by: Harold Cheatham

Dedication

This book is dedicated to my brother Elkin B. Smith Jr. No matter how many brotherhood organizations I belong to our relationship is the standard that I use to measure all other's. Your continued love, support, guidance, and friendship have given me a great example to follow and some huge footsteps to walk in. I love and thank you for all that you have done and continue to do for me.

Table of Contents

C. Talmadge Green

Coleman Talmadge Green had it all. At least he possessed all of the material items so many people are always chasing. He was well educated, a professional man. Gainfully employed as an accountant at one of the nations premiere accounting firms Arthur Anderson in downtown Chicago, Illinois. He had a six-figure income and was the recent recipient of a promotion, which came complete with a corner office on a high floor even though many others at the firm were being let go due to major restructuring. His skills, competence, and loyalty to the company made him a valuable asset to the firm.

He was married to Nancy. She was a slim, attractive, young woman he had met when he moved to Chicago to accept the position at the firm. During college Talmadge didn't have the confidence to date he was from a low-income family and focused his attention on getting the education essential to better his life. Talmadge and his wife had two beautiful children one girl and one boy. Talmadge wanted to have the idea American family and life. He lived in a sprawling, suburban estate of his own design in south suburban Chicago in an area called Country Club Hills.

Talmadge had designed his house to stand out in the community. His home had three levels, five bedrooms, a game room featuring a full bar which he had been using overtime in the past six months. His great room had vaulted ceilings, and was located on the main level of the home. Even the master

7

bedroom had vaulted ceilings. The homes main kitchen was huge. It had every amenity imaginable: marble countetops, dual ovens, and stainless steel appliances. The kitchen had been designed to be big enough to handle the king sized appetite of the giant sized man that Talmadge had become. He weighed some 300 plus pounds which packed his five foot ten inch frame into a mass that reminded all who saw him of the comic book villain "The Blob", who fought for Magneto's Brotherhood of Mutants in the famed X-Men comic book series. Talmadge rationalized his weight with the juvenile thought "big men have big successes, and deserve big things".

A large man with a large house also needed a large yard to go with it. Talmadge had purchased two lots to put his house on. He had a large yard complete with a large in-ground pool and a swing set for his children. All surrounded by a wooden privacy fence Talmadge had spared no expense in designing a home that would stand out in the community but would be kept sheltered from outside intrusion. Another unique feature of Talmadge's home was his deck-garage combination that he used to entertain his co-workers and friends, during the summer months. The garage was large enough to accommodate three and one half vehicles and had garage doors that opened on both the front and rear of the house giving one the ability to drive into the backyard from the front by going through the garage. Adjacent to the rear garage entrance was the first or ground level of the enormous deck. It was a grand platform that had bench style seating on three sides of the platform. A set of stairs led from the ground level to the upper level of the deck, which held the massive grill that Talmadge boasted, " was the largest anywhere in Chicago except for the one at Leon's Bar-b-q". It was not just a grill it was a complete outdoor kitchen. The joke among Talmadge's friends was that Talmadge had spent twice as much on his indoor and outdoor kitchens as he had on the rest of the house because being as large as he was he feared starving and always wanted to have direct access to food and the ability to feed himself instantly. He even had a special kitchenette added to his master bedroom while others in his sub-division had opted for the traditional seating area in the room. There was also the standard outdoor table complete with oversized umbrella to protect guest from the sun. The umbrella was another necessity for Talmadge who emitted an aroma of his last meal through his pores whenever he was exposed to the summer sunlight for too long. The odor that came from Talmadge never seemed to compliment the meal that he was cooking on the grill, nor the game of dominos, nor cards he often played at the table.

Despite Talmadge's pursuit, and possession of the absolute best his size always seemed to contradict his taste and styles. His home was spectacularly furnished with antiques. The interiors were filled with a variety of expensive paintings and one of a kind statues as well as the best and latest in electronic equipment - plasma screen televisions, remote controlled lights and window treatments. The entire house was wired for sound, computers, and satellite television all controllable via the Internet from anywhere in the world. His taste in clothes was impeccable. Yes, Talmadge was truly a walking contradiction. On the one hand he had labored so hard to amass these material possessions while on the other hand he was only one more hamburger away from a fatal heart attack or stroke. Despite his numerous successes, Talmadge always seemed to be searching for the next material item to possess. Some might suggest that his appetite for possessing the best that his money could buy was only surpassed by his appetite for food.

This obsession with possessing more and better was also reflected in his choice of automobiles as well. Talmadge owned a Mercedes Benz 500 C. Not the latest model but a 1994 edition, which has often been referred to as the quintessential collectors car by true car enthusiast. It did not matter that his oversized frame made the car look to be full of people even though he was riding alone. It was the status associated with having the car that Talmadge was interested in. He would be seen driving and owning a classic.

When Talmadge cared about driving a vehicle that was more accommodating for his behemoth physique he drove his other vehicle, a 2006 fully loaded custom Cadillac Escalade. It was pearl white and Talmadge had spared no expense in adding all of the creature comforts of home. He had televisions in the headrest and ceiling, a DVD player along with XM satellite radio and a stellar navigation system. Just like the two kitchens in his home, his truck was also equipped with a refrigerator and microwave. Talmadge had custom ordered the mini appliances. He said "it was for the kids" during those long family drives out of town to visit his mother in Rockford, Illinois. In reality a man of his size was always eating and drinking something and had to keep his supply handy. As a matter of fact, the mini refrigerator in the truck always contained more beer than beverages suitable for two young kids.

If being obsessed with material possessions was Talmadge's first vice, and his obsession with food his second, it was his ever, increasing love of alcohol which threatened to replace both of those within the next month. With everything he owned all the personal and professional success he gained it seemed he was always using alcohol to numb himself. Crown Royal, straight in a glass with a little ice was his favorite beverage. He kept a constant supply in all of his kitchens including the mini refrigerator in the Escalade. He kept so much on hand that he was suspected of having made a special deal with the liquor distributors in the area. Due to his weight he had to consume massively increasing amounts before he could feel the buzz that helped masque his pain and shortcomings. The pain that he had created from years of climbing the corporate ladder, the stress of being a husband, father, provider, collector, and keeper of secrets. Secrets he shared only with himself over a glass of Crown Royal or a case or two of beer.

Yes, Talmadge had it all, and he thought about it as he turned the ignition of his Escalade preparing for the long commute to his downtown Chicago office.

The Drive

Everyday the commute became just one more pressure to deal with. Working at a prestigious downtown accounting firm came with significant financial benefits, but living close to work was not one of them. The city was too crowded, too cramped, and too average for a man like Talmadge. He preferred life in the suburbs to escape living to close to the type of people he had worked so hard to get away from. Talmadge had grown up poor living around Blacks and other minorities. He had vowed early on in life to never again return to that lifestyle. He also vowed to never subject his children to the life he felt was reserved for minorities.

In a way this morning was no different from any other. Talmadge would cruise North on Interstate 57 until it merged with the Dan Ryan expressway, although there was seldom anything resembling express speed at this time of the morning. Rush hour in Chicago must have been named for the fact that everyone wanted to rush, but due to the large volume of traffic found themselves trapped in a virtual parade of morning commuters each snaking their way along the 5 lanes of concrete. However, traveling North on Interstate 57 was not too bad. From his home in Country Club Hills to the Dan Ryan merge at 95th street took an average of 15 minutes. Once there it would take him another 15 minutes to travel the roughly eight blocks to the

87th street exit where he would leave the slow pace of the expressway and play pole position through the city streets the remainder of the way to downtown Chicago. Talmadge opted for the same route each and every day. He had tried other routes over the years, but had found this one to be the best.

Turn right onto 87th down to King Drive, left onto King Drive and from there all the way to 22nd street. Talmadge often laughed to himself that it would be so ironic that the street he counted on to get him to work was named after a Black man that he himself had no desire to be associated with. As a matter of fact he had been quoted at a Republican fund raiser sponsored by his firm saying he "wished they change all of the Martin Luther King drives in this country to be named after a better example of minorities in this country like Supreme Court Justice Clarence Thomas. Now that's a drive I wouldn't mind taking everyday" he boasted as he touched glasses with the other guest at his table.

It was August 3rd, the weather was not going to cooperate with Talmadge's strict schedule. It had just started to rain. It was not pouring down but that light, misty, annoying type of rain. The type of rain that caused accidents by making the oil and other crud on the streets slick enough to keep the rubber on the tires from meeting the road.

Talmadge hadn't checked the weather the night before like he normally did. He had been out late at Griffis street bar and grill with a friend sipping drinks and talking about the problems she was having with her husband who was one of

14

Talmadge's fraternity brothers. As a result he had gotten home too late to see the nightly news. He hadn't adjusted his departure time to compensate for the cautious drivers who would slow down for safety at the slightest glimpse of rain. Talmadge had little patience. He had lived his life in a constant rush and something as mettlesome as rain was not going to impede his progress today. He was not going to walk into work later than 7:15 to start his 7:30 workday. "On time is 15 minutes early" he recalled his college career counselor saying to him once. This sage piece of advice he never forgot and had embraced it so thoroughly that he often found himself chastising his colleagues who did not share his regard for time.

Talmadge eased the Escalade out of the driveway backwards and then as if activating some type of warp drive shifted the truck into drive and sped off. The huge truck glided through the damp suburban streets as if it were a hovercraft from one of the Star Wars films. "It says stop, not park!" Talmadge exclaimed loudly to himself as he encountered the first of what he knew would be dozens of slow drivers impeding his progress. He was almost to the on ramp for Interstate 57 North when a police car pulled out in front of him from a Burger King driveway causing him to jam on the breaks. He was doing 50 mph on a damp side street where the posted speed limit was 30 mph. He did not need a ticket this early in the morning from an overzealous radar gun toting, breakfast sandwich eating, suburban cop. One right turn later he was headed North on

15

Interstate 57 barreling across all four lanes of traffic in search of that prized spot in the far left hand lane. There with his high beams and fog lights burning he would exceed the 55 mph speed limit in spite of the rain damped pavement and risky driving conditions. His customized grill daring those in front of him to speed in order to lead or be ran over. Most drivers intimidated by the huge custom chrome grill and excessively bright lights simply moved aside rather than be in his way.

Talmadge relished every time another car relinquished their lead and moved right, it proved that he had in deed purchased a powerful car worth every penny he had spent. He looked at the dashboard clock and thought "I am making decent time but I am still a few minutes behind my norm". He pressed a little harder on the gas pedal and smiled an evil grin as the engine of the Escalade responded to his non-verbal demand for more speed. The engine purred a little louder and cars that were at least a quarter of a mile ahead of him moved right to clear a path in anticipation of Talmadge's Escalade bearing down on them. 127th, 119th, 99th, the streets kept flying past until finally the traffic began to slow and then to crawl. Talmadge saw the 95th street elevated train station and instinctively slowed to a snails pace to match the traffic that he was merging into. He now began the tremendous task of moving across what was now becoming six lanes of traffic trying to force his way right so he could escape from the mass congestion at the 87th street exit.

Fifteen minutes later he was cruising up the exit ramp

heading for 87th street and a date with destiny. Just as he reached the end of the ramp and was preparing to merge right so that he could turn onto 87th street, a black Escalade with a huge custom grill and lights blaring came flying out of nowhere almost sideswiping Talmadge. The black Escalade forced Talmadge to curse, swerve, and stop all in the same moment.

"Son of a B****!" Talmadge yelled, but the expletive did nothing to slow the black Escalade that had just rolled by. Talmadge recovered jerking his truck left then swerving back to the right into the right turning lane. The black Escalade was now directly in front of him with its right turn signal flashing as if mocking Talmadge with each, amber flash and annoying click. Of course, Talmadge did not actually hear the clicking of the other Escalades turn signal, it was the blaring click of his own turn signal, and the "no turn on red" sign that had him trapped and taunted. The one thing Talmadge hated more than slow drivers was impetuous speedsters who cut him off, and Mr. black Escalade had done just that. It did not help that the black Escalade was sitting on a set of super expensive rims that Talmadge had just ordered believing he would be the first if not the only person to have this particular set of rims on an Escalade.

The light seemed to sit on red for an eternity. With each passing second Talmadge became more and more infuriated. The light turned green and both Escalades jumped into action. Each shooting through the right turn as if being guided by a raised metal strip like the one on a child's racecar set. Down 87th street they ran. It was only six blocks to King Drive from the Dan Ryan expressway, but Talmadge was determined not to spend those few blocks behind this guy who had just cut him off. What Talmadge did not realize was that the driver of the black Escalade was just as determined to stay in front of him.

Talmadge whipped into the right lane and began to accelerate, hoping to position himself to be able to pass the black Escalade at the stop sign that was now just one block away. The black Escalade countered by not completely stopping at the stop sign. He merely slowed and then accelerated through the sign forcing Talmadge to have to stop to avoid an accident. Talmadge not to be outdone stopped for a microsecond then immediately took off veering left to regain his position behind the black Escalade avoiding the cars that were parked in the right lane ahead of him. This further frustrated Talmadge as he approached King Drive still in second place. He was going to have to admit defeat this time. His turn onto King Drive was coming up and he had no hope of passing the black Escalade before then. Talmadge could not believe what he was seeing. It was as if someone were playing a cruel joke on him. The black Escalade moved into the left turn lane ahead of him, it too was going to be heading North on King Drive. Talmadge steamed at the thought of having to remain behind the black Escalade for a longer period. His temperature began to rise and in an air-conditioned truck Talmadge began to sweat.

As they both sat waiting for the light to turn green

Talmadge tried to size his opponent up. He tried to see what this reckless driving guy looked like by looking at his face in the driver's side mirror. It was to no avail. The tint on the driver's side window of the black Escalade was too dark. It was limousine black and impossible to see through just like the tint on the rear of the truck. Talmadge couldn't see a thing. He couldn't even see the street in front of him through the deep tinted glass. The thought of not being able to see his nemesis frustrated Talmadge even more.

"Just another raggedy rap music playing Nigger", Talmadge thought without the slightest sense of remorse for using a racial epithet. As if being given a cue Talmadge felt the windows in his Escalade rattle from the heavy bass thumps resonating from the black Escalade as its driver increased the volume on the trucks powerful stereo. It was so loud that Talmadge felt every word the young rap lyricist was saying, even though he could not understand them. Talmadge hated rap music, rappers and in his mind the "niggers" who made it and played it. Sweat running down his face, heart rate pounding and anger steadily rising, Talmadge flipped up the armrest in his Escalades center panel revealing the mini-fridge and grabbed a beer.

The light turned green and Talmadge punched the gas then immediately stabbed on the break. The black Escalade ahead of him had not moved. Every morning Talmadge had timed this light so that he turned in front of the oncoming traffic

19

before they could move. Today the black Escalade in front of him kept him from using his patented move. The huge black Escalade sat there allowing the traffic to proceed the way it should, yielding the right of way to those who legally deserved it.

The light turned yellow and the oncoming traffic slowed, and then stopped giving the black Escalade the right away, it did not move until the light turned red. By waiting for the light to turn red before moving through the intersection Mr. black Escalade forced Talmadge to miss the light and was now speeding North on King Drive with Talmadge and his white Escalade fading into a distant memory. Talmadge sensing what was happening immediately leaned into his horn. He lit into it like a prizefighter swinging his arms warming up for a big fight. It was no use the black Escalade was cruising North down King Drive.

A split second before the light turned green again Talmadge tore through the intersection making his left turn before the oncoming traffic could budge. The tires of his Escalade screamed as Talmadge pressed down on the accelerator with one thought in his mind - to catch up to the black Escalade. As Talmadge traveled North on King Drive the mist increased to a small rainstorm. His wipers dancing across the windshield, and headlights blaring both seemed to be scanning the horizon in search of a glimpse of the black Escalade. It was not until he had reached 79th street that Talmadge saw the black Escalade ahead of him. By the time he reached 76th street Talmadge had driven in the oncoming traffic to pass two slower moving cars and was now positioned behind the Escalade again. "I'll teach you to make me miss the light," Talmadge said aloud while putting the finishing touches on his second can of beer.

The two trucks and their masters continued their game of hot pursuit with the black Escalade always managing to stay ahead of Talmadge. Talmadge's only focus was to get in front of the black truck that had passed him. Getting to work on time became secondary. "No one beats me, no one" Talmadge thought his eyes glossing as he reached for his third beer in less than five minutes. "71st street is my best spot" Talmadge strategized to himself. "I will pass him on the right hand side".

The two cars cruised towards 71st street. They could both see that the light on 71st and King Drive was already red stopping traffic in their direction. King Drive was really a four-lane street, two lanes of traffic going North and two lanes of traffic going South. However the zoning laws allowed people to park their cars in the far right lanes in both directions effectively reducing the street to two lanes in some spots. The only time parking was not allowed was in the winter if two or more inches of snow had fallen. But it was not winter, there was no snow in Chicago in August, and cars were parked on King Drive this morning.

The stretch of road between 73rd street and 71st street on King Drive was void of apartments or houses in the northbound lanes. Talmadge always used this stretch of road to get around slower drivers when he was on his way to work. He used the right lane as his own personal drag strip always passing on the right hand side. Today he knew it would bring him victory over his unsuspecting but annoying foe. For the two short blocks both vehicles traveled side-by-side increasing their speed in anticipation that the light ahead would change to green by the time they arrived.

Faster and faster they both went neither willing to give the other an inch to get ahead. The two trucks dominated the two lanes so completely that there was barely three inches separating the mirrors of each vehicle from one another.

They were both traveling in excess of 60 miles per hour in a 30 mile per hour zone. Both drivers locked in a battle. Road rage was gone she had been angrily replaced by her father, road war. On the North side of 71st street and King Drive sitting in the right hand lane was a delivery truck dropping off a fresh supply of firewater to be sold at the only type of establishment that seemed to flourish in this community - a liquor store. The two speeding monsters would have little room to maneuver or stop if need be.

As the two marauding vehicles approached the intersection, the light just as expected did indeed turn green, but not before a Chicago Transit Authority bus barreled through the intersection coming from the West completing a left hand turn onto King Drive. Both North bound lanes were now completely blocked, one by the delivery truck the other by a bus.

Carlos Hosey

The driver of the black Escalade was the first to realize the impending danger and desperately tried to stop his vehicle from colliding with the bus. He was unable to pull into the right lane because of Talmadge; he then tried to turn left onto 71st street hoping to avoid hitting the rear of the bus. The force of the turn proved to be too much for the speeding truck. It swerved left on two wheels, somersaulting in mid-air three times before it came to rest on top of the city bus and burst into flames.

Talmadge's attempts at stopping were equally in vain. Trapped to his left by the black Escalade and to his right by sidewalks, street poles, and pedestrians he could not avoid the delivery truck in front of him. Tires screeching, Talmadge struck the delivery truck with such force that he was ejected from the Escalade. Due to his size Talmadge never wore a seat belt even though he had had his custom enlarged to accommodate his oversized frame. Talmadge's body hit the delivery truck at the exact same time as the truck burst into flames from the impact of his Escalade. The resulting blast combined with the explosion from the bus and the black Escalade propelled Talmadge head first through the liquor store window. Alcohol bottles exploded in midair then fell back to Earth showering the ground with a mixture of rain, glass and alcohol. The delivery truck, the storefront, a city bus and two Escalades were all burning wildly.

It took three firefighting units from across the city four hours to get the inferno under control, tend to the wounded, and retrieve the bodies. Talmadge had surely died in the blast or the resulting flames. For all that he possessed immortality was still out of reach for Talmadge, or was it?

"What's going on?" inquired a dazed and confused Talmadge pointing at the scene of the fire and rescue personnel. The figure seated near Talmadge was a thin and dressed in a gray suit. His face was hidden, buried in a book of some sort. He did not respond to Talmadge's question. In fact he did not acknowledge Talmadge at all. Talmadge slowly lifted his body mass up and began to walk toward the figure. As he approached the man the scene around Talmadge shifted, and suddenly the man was gone.

Talmadge took inventory of his new surroundings. He was no longer on the corner of 71st and King Drive. He was surrounded by lush trees, and a few buildings with manicured lawns, and pristine side walks in front of them. It all looked familiar to him but he was still a little dazed and confused.

"Mr. Green" a voice called out from behind him.

Talmadge turned to find a young Marine with a disfigured face standing at arms length away from him. The young Marine had a skeletal outline and bone structure but his face was bloody and his uniform torn as if he had just been in a battle. He even had small medal fragments protruding from several places in his body. "What's wrong Cheese, don't you

24

remember me?"

Talmadge was disgusted by the soldiers' appearance and quickly tried to turn away from the soldier. He had not been called "Cheese" since college and even then only by a select group of people. His fraternity brothers thought it would be a good nickname for him. They actually called him Limburger Cheese because of his robustness, pale complexion and strange but putrid odor. He shortened it to just Cheese when he was in public trying to make it pass for a more respectable nickname. "How could this disfigured person know me?" he wondered. "Who are you?" he asked, not really wanting to know the answer.

The scenery changed again, Talmadge and the young Marine were now inside a classroom. The desk seemed like doll furniture next to Talmadge's enormous body. With a dumbstruck awe Talmadge first recognized the classroom and finally the Marine who stood before him.

"This is my introductory accounting seminar classroom. You were in my class. You were one of the two blacks who were in my class".

"One of the two blacks? Is that what you thought about us? My name is Sergeant Carlos Hosey. My friends in the core called me Deuce. They say that I was a wild man so that I needed a wild nickname to match my actions. Since we are not friends and with that gut you could never make it in the core, you can call me Mr. Hosey."

Talmadge's eyes hung low. A flood of memories from his collegiate days came running back to him. He had always referred to Carlos Hosey as "one of the two black guys" in the class. He even went as far as to make a distinction between the two black guys in the class, always-identifying Carlos as "the other black guy". In fact when they were assigned to be in a group together in the course he joked with the other students in the group that he wished "the other black guy could be in the other group". Talmadge recalled that the one group project was worth 90% of a student's grade in the course. It was also the course, which determined if one would be allowed to remain an accounting major. Failing the course would result in the student being dismissed from the accounting program due to its highly competitive nature.

Once the groups had been assigned Talmadge took offense to the fact that a black student had been placed in a group with him. He didn't want him in the group, and had even gone as far as to see the professor to see if he could get "the other black guy" reassigned to another group. When the professor had made it clear that Carlos Hosey was going to remain in the group as long as he did his share of the work, Talmadge began plotting on how to get rid of him.

"I see it's all coming back to you now, hey Cheesy boy? You are thinking about that group project aren't you?" The young Marine said turning his mutilated head to face Talmadge. The young Marine smiled as he began to recount the story of the group project.

"You know I actually felt honored to be in a group with you. Based on your participation in class I knew you understood the material, and would not be a slacker." A cigarette appeared in the Marines right hand. It was as if he had willed it to appear out of thin air. He didn't light it but it was burning. He placed the brown tip to his lip and took a long drag causing the amber tip to glow a bright red and drop ash to the floor. He exhaled and a cloud of smoke exited his mouth as he continued to talk to Talmadge.

"For some reason, I was never able to figure out you just never did like me. At first it didn't bother me I just took it as part of the academic rights of passage. Then it just seemed to get really personal. Remember when you deliberately told me the wrong time for our group meeting? I showed up and you all were done meeting. I felt stupid and thought you would just tell everyone that you gave me the wrong time but you didn't. Instead you lied and tried to make me look like a slacker."

Talmadge was becoming more uncomfortable under the Marines glare. It was something about his disfigured face that unnerved Talmadge. It made the young Marines words seem to cut him that much deeper. It made the young Marine appear to be fierce, almost as if he was engaged in a battle with Talmadge.

Talmadge stepped forward in a feeble attempt to cut off the words of Carlos Hosey, but the young Marine was not going to be denied his say.

"Now don't blame me for your lack of timeliness" Talmadge snapped.

"Lack of timeliness!" barked Carlos back at him while taking another drag on his cigarette. "How dare you sit here now and still refuse to admit the truth. You don't get it do you? The reason you are here right now is to face the truth of your life. You can't handle the truth," he said laughing. " I have always wanted to say that to someone. You see I am but the first, if you can't deal with me I know you are not ready for what is to come. I hope we will be never see each other again after this but based on your unwillingness to admit the truth, we probably will see each other again real soon."

Talmadge's head dropped. All he could think about was how bad he wanted a drink. What he wouldn't do to be able to make a beer appear in his hand just as Carlos had done with the cigarette. He even looked at his watch checking to see how late he would be for work. Simultaneously something inside of him was telling him not to worry about work. Being late was the least of his worries today the inner voice told him.

"Don't worry about the time. You have all of the time you will need. As a matter of fact that is exactly what you told me after mysteriously misplacing my portion of our final report for the group project. You told me I had all of the time I needed to retype all fourteen pages. Perhaps if we had gone to college in the age of the personal computer I could have typed it all over. But we didn't we were still using manual type writers, and you waited until the very last minute to tell me you had misplaced my part of the report. You even went so far as to tell the professor that I had not submitted anything. You said that you and the rest of the group had to do my share of the report. It was quite the setup. It seems that no one trusted "the other black guy" and I ended up failing the course because of yours and the other group members' evaluation of my participation in the project. I even got put out of the accounting program altogether."

The Young Marine flicked his cigarette in Talmadge's direction, and moved closer to him. A look of anger overcame him as his body tensed and his fist began to clutch and form a ball he continued with his story.

"You don't know what your little scheme cost me do you?"

Talmadge became immediately defensive. He positioned his massive frame as if readying to fight. He stepped back giving himself a little distance from the angered Marine before speaking. "I said it's not my fault you didn't do your work. You almost made us get a failing grade! The truth is I did you a favor." Talmadge sensing his words were just further aggravating the Marine searched for the right words to diffuse the situation but also looked for items he could use as a weapon if he indeed had to fight him. "I checked the report and it was full of errors. I could not turn that in. I tried to cover for you but the others in the group would not let me. They were the ones who told the professor you did not pull your share of weight."

"Now Talmadge, we both know that is a lie" Carlos interrupted. He had somehow managed to maneuver himself behind Talmadge. His left hand pressing on Talmadge's shoulder and his right hand waving in a circular motion in front of them changing the classroom into what now resembled a college professors tiny book filled office. They both watched as a young Talmadge sat talking with His Accounting Professor.

"You see Dr. Petty the other black guy you put in our group is different. He has done nothing but hold our group back. It would be unfair for you to give him a passing grade based on the work the rest of us completed. The group has asked me to talk to you about this."

"This is what you call speaking on my behalf?" Carlos asked sarcastically pressing the issue with Talmadge. Before Talmadge could respond the Marine waved his hand and the scene changed again. Now they were sitting in a sparsely decorated apartment. It was a dimly lit room that lacked adequate lighting, but everything else about the place said order. There were two men sitting at a kitchen table. Talmadge recognized one of them as a younger Carlos Hosey dressed in blue jeans and a state college sweatshirt. The other gentleman was dressed in a khaki blue work suit that had a name patch over the right breast and the company name "Republic Steel" over the left chest. When he raised his head to eat Talmadge could clearly see that he looked like an older more powerful version of Carlos.

"That's my old man," said Carlos as if he could read the

confusion in Talmadge's face. "This is the day my grades came home along with the letter stating that I was no longer an accounting major. You need to see and hear this" Carlos stated as he motioned for Talmadge to look at the scene.

"I am not working this hard to send you to college so you can fail a class!" yelled Carlos's father.

"But pops" interjected Carlos to no avail.

"Don't interrupt me boy. If you are not majoring in accounting then you are not wasting any more of my money at that school. I told you, you was going to that school to learn a profession. You supposed to be an accountant, you know something respectable. People always gone have money and they gone always have to have someone to count it and pay taxes. I don't want you rotting away in some steel mill like me. Now look at this letter you done messed up, gone and got yourself kicked out of your future. I think you need to learn some responsibility the old way. You are going to the Marines. They helped make me a responsible man and they can do the same for you."

The scene faded to black and Talmadge could see a tear fall down Carlos's face. "The next day I went and enlisted in the United States Marine Corp," A reflective Carlos recounted as he stared off into the darkness.

"I knew I never saw you around after that class, but I had no ideal what had happened to you" Talmadge said in a rather smug tone.

"To be honest you didn't care what had happened to me either did you?" Carlos snapped back. "I joined the Corp and was quickly promoted to Sergeant right in time for the first Gulf War. I was in a Bradley fighting vehicle when we were attacked. I was killed in that battle. A battle I should probably never have been in." Another cigarette appeared in his hand and the two men were instantly transported into an open field of green. Sergeant Carlos Hosey was now walking away from Talmadge.

" I had hoped you and I would never meet again, I had hoped that you would have changed. Unfortunately based on our time together I am sure we will meet again." Carlos said his voice fading as he walked away.

With that being said Sergeant Carlos Hosey disappeared into the horizon. A small trail of smoke slipped into the sky, and a cigarette butt still blazing dropped at Talmadge's feet as if it had been thumped at him from the disappearing Marine.

Talmadge tried to run after Carlos. His weight and the slight incline of the green field made that an impossible task. He took four steps and slumped over gasping for air. He might as well have tried to run a marathon, the effects of that short jaunt was too much for his out of shape body to bear. He called out "wait" but it was too late. He was alone.

Glenda Jean Spencer

Talmadge rested a moment trying to ponder what had just transpired. Caught in the memories of his undergraduate experiences, he was confused. He did not understand where he was, or even when it was for that matter. He glanced at his watch and it was still showing the same time it had when he was talking to Carlos. "That's odd," he said aloud.

"Not really" said a female voice from behind. Talmadge turned around startled by the voice.

As he turned around to see who had spoken to him it was clear that he was no longer standing in a grassy field. He was now in the midst of an office building surrounded by a maze of cubicles. He looked down to see a very small black woman with salt and pepper hair. Her uniform resembled that of a maid, but this was no house it was an office building. Suddenly Talmadge recognized his surroundings and the lady. He was on the 34th floor of the Arthur Anderson building - his place of employment. Looking at his watch again he smiled "I made it on time after all. This is the wrong floor but hey at least I am on time." He paused and looked around again and saw that he and the cleaning woman were the only people on the floor - something was wrong. "This is the floor I used to work on," he said. He took a few steps forward as the elderly woman disappeared into one of the larger cubicles. Talmadge followed and found her dutifully

33

dusting the industrialized desk and computer monitor with a feather duster. She dusted the nameplate on the desk, and then repositioned it on the corner of the desk next to a gold business card holder and clock like the ones you see in the mall at the "Things Remembered" store. The nameplate read "Coleman Talmadge Green".

"This is my old desk," Talmadge declared both excited by the familiarity but confused by it as well. Shaking his head he spoke aloud "Perhaps I am not losing my mind after all".

"Of course you are not Mr. Green," stated the cleaning woman as she moved to dump the trash from the waste can into a larger bag on her cleaning cart. "You have not lost your mind, but your common sense and your soul is another story" she quipped.

"Lady do you know who I am? I could have your job for talking to me like that." Talmadge barked as he walked into the cubicle and sat at his old desk glaring at the old woman as if he expected her to acknowledge his last statement with an apology.

"I know who you are Mr. Green, and you have already had me fired. None of that makes what I said any less true. How else do you explain coming to work smelling of and drinking alcohol? If you had any common sense you would have known better. If you had a soul it would have told you better." Talmadge sat straight up in the chair looking around to make sure no one else had heard the accusations that the old cleaning woman was throwing around. "You'd better watch yourself old woman",

Talmadge spoke in a deep malicious whisper.

"Or what?" asked the woman without breaking her cleaning routine. "You don't scare me. How soon do we forget hey Mr. Green? You get moved up one floor, and all of the sudden your memory gets bad." The cleaning woman turned to face Talmadge, she placed the feather duster back on her cleaning cart and looked him in his eye and scowled "After all I have done for you this is the best you can do in return threaten to fire me - again? I had hoped you had changed, I guess I should be grateful that you at least have the guts to say it to my face this time." Talmadge sat back in the chair as he tried to search the recesses of his mind. "Do I know this woman? Why does she keep saying I have already fired her? If I did fire her why is she still here working? It just doesn't make sense." Talmadge was struggling searching the recesses of his mind for clues as to who this woman was.

"I see you don't recognize me," the cleaning woman said. "It is funny how some people get a little uppity, and forget where they came from. That's why we're here you know... help you with your memory problem." The woman walked toward Talmadge and leaned her five feet one inch frame over the desk looking Talmadge straight in his eyes and with the conviction of a mother said "You should be ashamed of yourself Mr. Green. You know what is done in the dark will come to the light."

The cubicle darkened, the desk and the computer disappeared and were replaced with a long corridor and a bank of elevators. There in front of the elevators stood another younger Talmadge. The elevator door opened revealing the cleaning woman pushing her cart out of the elevator through the open doors. The younger Talmadge entered the elevator nearly running her over as he impatiently tried to maneuver his massive frame past her cart as she was exiting. His 60-inch waste pressed up against her cart forcing the elevator doors to remain open.

"Good evening Mr. Green," the cleaning woman said speaking to the younger Talmadge as he was entering the elevator. She seemed unable to see her double and the other Talmadge who were there observing the incident. It was all surreal to Talmadge as if he was reliving the event not actually watching it. The characters in each memory acting just as they had acted only this time he was privy to seeing it all without himself being seen. The younger Talmadge entered the elevator and looked to see who had spoken to him. Realizing that it was only the cleaning lady he quickly decided that she was not worth him returning the courtesy of a simple greeting. He pushed the button for the lobby and waited for the doors to close never once acknowledging her in any fashion. This scene continued to repeat itself. Each time the two characters seemed to age before Talmadge's eyes. Each time Talmadge never spoke to the woman regardless of how many times she spoke to him. Oddly the woman regardless of how many times she ignored politely greeted Talmadge every time their paths crossed. "How many times are we going to have to watch the same thing?"

36

Talmadge asked frustrated by the scenes apparent repetition. "It is not repeating each of these is a different day, covering multiple years of your working at this company. In ten years you have only spoken to me once.

The scene changed again and they found themselves in a large office with windows and a remarkable view of Michigan Avenue, Lake Michigan, and the Chicago skyline. Seated in a massive leather chair was a young Talmadge. Directly across from him behind a huge mahogany desk in an even larger leather chair with a high back sat Dennis Weis, Senior Partner of Arthur Anderson. Seated on the same side of the desk as Talmadge but to his right was Lucy Waters Director of Human Resources for Arthur Anderson. Dennis Weis was your typical looking White man in height and weight but his face displayed a youthful image that one would not expect to see on a senior executive of a fortune 500 company. He was called the Mark Cuban of the financial world, because he looked more like the kind of guy you would see sitting at a basketball game in jeans instead of a $3,000.00 business suit. Some associates at Arthur Anderson had even lost their jobs for making jokes about the partners while on the elevator or in the lobby not knowing that the average looking guy standing near them was indeed one of the power brokers they were making light of. If the other associates at Arthur Anderson had Talmadge's eye for fashion they would have been able to tell from the fine Persian wool of his suits, or the hand spun silk in his imported ties that Mr. Weis was far from an average associate. Mr. Weis was far from average when it came to his wardrobe. Diamond studded cuff links with a matching lapel pin, Cole Hahn shoes all staples in his attire. In fact it was his style of dress that Talmadge was trying to emulate. "Dress to the level you aspire to rise to at the company, not the level you are at" Talmadge recalled the career counselor saying.

Ms. Lucy Waters' was an equally impressive dresser. Her ability to find shoes and accessories that matched exactly was often the talk of the water cooler by female employees who were envious of Ms. Water's penchant for fashion. Her petite frame and toned physique made every outfit look as if it had been exclusively designed to her specifications. She too, like Mr. Weis carried her age well; she was 46 and unashamed of it. She wore her hair in a very short natural, and had recently died it blonde which gave her a runway-fierce look that complimented her caramel brown skin tone. She had worked her way up the corporate ladder through hard work and dedication, starting out as a secretary and taking classes at night earning her degree in three years and graduating in the top of her class. Everyone at Arthur Anderson knew her story, and respected her accomplishments. She had earned the human resources position in part because in her sixteen years of service, she always treated everyone with respect. It made no difference to her if you worked in the mailroom or the boardroom, a janitor, or an executive "Everyone has worth" she would say and "my job is to honor and respect that even when some people don't honor and respect it in themselves."

Talmadge had not spoken to her since his initial interview. He made it a habit to avoid fraternizing with the black employees regardless of their position. Although he never would ignore Ms. Waters like he had ignored the cleaning lady, he viewed both in the same negative light that he viewed all of the black people he had come into contact with. "People to be avoided, less they bring you down". Talmadge felt awkward being seated across from Ms. Waters now. One thing she had made clear from their first meeting was that she was proud to be black and working in corporate America at the level she was. She was too proud to sacrifice her blackness to stay in that position as well.

Talmadge glanced at the cleaning lady and thought it odd that this was the scene he was being forced to relive with the cleaning lady. A huge lump gathered in Talmadge's throat, as he looked back at the scene and mumbled to the cleaning lady "Why are we here?"

"Just watch" the cleaning lady rebutted as she directed his attention to the scene in the room.

Ms. Waters peered over the top of her Anne Kline eyeglasses parted her lips and began with, "Mr. Green we are here to follow-up on a concern that we have which may or may not affect your employment here with Arthur Anderson. You may choose not to answer the questions we pose, but that will be viewed as your unwillingness to cooperate with an internal investigation and based on the terms of your employment contract would be grounds for immediate termination. Are you ready to proceed?"

The Talmadge seated across from Ms. Waters nodded his head in agreement and with that Mr. Weis began to speak. "Talmadge I like you but someone has complained that you have been drinking on the job. Before you answer you should know that we have even gone so far as to have your supervisor search your cubicle and trash. We did find some empty alcohol containers in your trash and now we want to know - what's going on? If you have a problem with alcohol we can get you some help."

Talmadge sat silently in the leather chair for a moment, cleared his throat and then directed his attention directly to Mr. Weis intentionally avoiding direct eye contact with Ms. Waters. "Mr. Weis this is so embarrassing, I must apologize" Talmadge began.

"Apologize for what?" interjected Ms. Waters who had never really gotten a positive vibe from Talmadge especially when he refused to participate in the black employee affinity group Anderson had begun. Now here he was involved in a drinking scandal at work, which would surely cast a shadow over the other black employees that would remain after he was fired.

"I had hoped to never have to discuss this. I am really truly, embarrassed. The alcohol containers are not mine" and with that being said Talmadge stopped talking and smiled at Mr.

Weis, still ignoring Ms. Waters.

"Is that all you have to say Talmadge?" asked Mr. Weis who sat waiting for more of a detailed explanation from his employee. "I mean your supervisor retrieved the containers from the cleaning lady after she emptied your waste basket, for God's sake how do you explain that?" Weis continued.

"Yes Mr. Green how do you explain that?" Ms. Waters stated, this time with a noticeable inflection in her voice and shift in her posture, which indicated her losing patience with Talmadge and his blatantly disrespectful attempts at ignoring her. Talmadge was indeed ignoring her. He was afraid that she might see through his plan if he made eye contact with her before getting his lie out.

"As I said this is embarrassing. I came back to work late one night to find the cleaning woman sitting in my cube having a beverage...if you know what I mean. She tried to hide it at first but the bottle clang when she dropped it in the bag with the other trash."

"I'm sorry what did you just say" erupted Ms. Waters who was now on the edge of her chair. "Do you expect us to believe that the cleaning woman is responsible for drinking in your cubicle?" Talmadge glanced to his right slightly trying to keep his eyes on Mr. Weis and fain-acknowledging Ms. Waters and retorted, "you don't think that I would be drinking on the job do you? I am not that dumb." No sooner had he finished the sentence than a huge knot rose up through his throat forcing him to gulp or risk throwing up from a combination of nervousness and the crown royal he had consumed before the meeting.

"How dumb you are remains to be seen" fired back Ms. Waters.

"Wait a minute Lucy, lets hear him out. Talmadge has been an exceptional worker. There was one incident early on with him being involved in a fight outside of work, but that was considered self-defense. The Supervisor did say he found her trying to hide the bottles while exiting Talmadge's office one night didn't he?" asked Mr. Weis looking for agreement from his human resources Director.

Talmadge had achieved the reasonable doubt from Mr. Weis he was hoping for, now he had to lay it on just a little thicker and this would be over before happy hour. "I don't mean to get anyone in trouble but I am not going to take the blame for something I did not do. I've worked too hard to get here. I've got too much to loose for a drunken black woman who cleans office buildings for a living." Talmadge said defensively. His voiced cracked as he continued to plead his case with the executives. After several heated exchanges between he and Ms. Waters, accompanied by a scolding glare from her indicating her disbelief of all that he had said Talmadge was excused from the office. The scene faded to darkness again, Talmadge turned around to find the cleaning lady hard at work dusting file cabinets. They had returned to the maze of cubicles. The cleaning woman was emptying the small wastebaskets into a larger wastebasket on her rolling cart. Each time she dumped a trashcan beer cans and other alcohol containers fell into her large cart. The rattling and crashes of the bottles did not go unnoticed by Talmadge.

"They fired me," she said not breaking her stride of emptying and cleaning. "Just called me in Mr. Weis did, and asked me had I seen the alcohol bottles in the trash. I thought they were coming after you so said I hadn't noticed alcohol bottles, just a bunch of trash. He thanked me for coming in and fired me right after that. Told me to go see Ms. Waters. Ms. Waters tried to defend me but Mr. Weis was not having it. I guess he figured it was easier to replace some black cleaning lady than to replace one of his accountants. Two months after that I lost my apartment, and was put out on the streets. It was February and quite cold round here. I thought I would be okay. I had my box and some newspaper to keep the cold off. I laid down that cold night, and I never woke up. "

Talmadge's knees buckled, he looked at the cleaning woman and tried to talk. "I thought they would just reassign you, move you to another floor to clean or something simple. Maybe suspend you for a few days, but I never thought they would fire you. You are a black woman - a cleaning lady. Who cares if you have a few drinks on the clock? It's not like you had a major role around here like monitoring someone's accounts or anything important. No one even saw you drinking; they can't fire you without proof. I am sure your lawyer will have a field day with this." The old cleaning lady lifted her head and looked at Talmadge. Her glance asking the question without her having to say a word "do I look like I could have afforded a lawyer to fight this?"

Talmadge answered the unspoken question aloud "I guess you probably don't have or can't afford a lawyer huh? I am sure they knew that when they fired you. It's not right they should not have done you that way. They should not have fired you!" Talmadge completed his ramblings and then he felt a disturbing chill. He felt alone. He looked up and he was alone.

He turned and looked in every direction, the old cleaning lady had simply disappeared. He noticed that his surroundings had changed again as well. He was no longer trapped in the maze of cubicles. Nor was he back in Mr. Weis's office. He was no longer at work. "Noooo!" he screamed before finding himself seated in a booth instead of a cubicle. The room was dimly lit and the smell of Mexican çuisine filled the air making his oversized mouth wet with saliva from just the mere thought of eating. The sound of sports and music echoed in the background, as if coming from some distant television and jukebox.

Talmadge did not recognize the place he seemed disoriented. Just moments ago he had thought his nightmare was over. He hoped that he might have been waking from some drunken stew safe and sound at his place of employment. He began to slide his wide body sideways in order to release himself from the confines of the booth. Suddenly, a hand reached out of the darkness from behind him and gently touched his shoulder. "Not leaving so soon I hope?" a woman's voice whispered.

Teresa Sapphire

Talmadge looked over his shoulder and was immediately frightened. The last person he ever expected, or even wanted to see was standing over him on the outside of the booth. His legs collapsed and his body dropped a few inches plummeting his body back into the vinyl and wood booth. His eyes were stretched wide open, and his mouth was even wider, but Talmadge was unable to speak.

A short woman emerged from the darkened edge of the room sliding into the booth across from Talmadge. She was a five feet three inches tall, fair complexioned black woman. She had shoulder length brown hair with highlights that helped accent her petite face. Her dress and demeanor said "professional and educated". The way she moved into view with the dignity and stride of a debutante would bring to mind images of Whitney Gilbert from the "Cosby" show spin-off "A Different World". As she sat down you could tell that she was only a fraction of the woman she had once been. She was thin, a sickly thin, the type of weight loss one undergoes from being hospitalized. The black pants and purple shirt she wore fit loosely and did nothing to flatter her. Still something about the way she carried herself made her appear to be - special.

Talmadge may have been unsure about where he was but one thing was clear he knew this woman. She had been seated a few minutes before he got the nerve to look at her and say, "Teresa, I'm a little"…"Shocked, and surprised to see me? I bet you are. She said as she glared at him from across the booth. "Have you figured out where we are yet?" she asked with a sarcastic smile beaming from her face. "This is Muggsy's," she said feinting the excitement of a high school cheerleader. "This was our, - no I am sorry your on private playboy clubhouse. I used to think of it as our special place. The place it all began for us. I used to think that until I finally woke up and realized what a low down trifling dog you really are." Her teeth were now gritted and though she kept a smile on her face the tone in her voice was clear she was speaking to a man she now hated.

Muggsy's bar and grill was an out of the way sports bar that served Mexican cuisine but was known for their hot wings. It used to represent the edge of the city limits until a few years ago when they built a new subdivision surrounding the bar. Now it was an out of the way place that one could go and discreetly meet and eat in a casual atmosphere. Talmadge looked around and shook his head with recognition acknowledging that this indeed was his stomping ground. It was indeed the place he had first arranged to meet secretly Teresa. Talmadge liked Muggsy's because it was the type of place that few people who knew Talmadge or his wife would ever gather there, more importantly even fewer blacks would ever venture into. Teresa sarcastically commenting, "this brings back so many memories for me," interrupted Talmadge's reminiscing." Some I am still trying desperately to forget. How's your memory doing lover?" she quipped.

Talmadge obviously annoyed by the remark snapped back "My memories are just fine I am glad that you are concerned." "Don't flatter yourself" was Teresa's comeback. "I stopped being concerned about you the moment I left the doctors office," she said pointing her finger at Talmadge.

No sooner than she had uttered the words "doctors office", the scene changed to that of a doctor's office. The two of them were no longer seated in a booth at Muggsy's, but were now both standing side-by-side looking on as a younger and much healthier Teresa waiting for the doctor to enter the room.

"What are we doing here?" demanded Talmadge. "You missed out on this experience the first time. I wanted you to see first hand what it was like for me to go through this all by myself", Teresa said sternly. She lifted her French manicured finger to her mouth and pressed it to her lips signaling Talmadge to be silent and listen as the doctor entered the room.

The doctor entered the room looked Teresa in the eye and in a somber tone began, "Well Ms. Sapphire you did the right thing coming down here. I am glad that you were able to get away from the school today. Based on the symptoms you gave me fatigue, weight loss, hemorrhoids, being unable to fight off infections and colds I ran a battery of test. I am afraid it is exactly what I feared. There is no easy way to say this but Teresa you have H.I.V. and it has developed into A.I.D.S. I'm sorry.

Your immune system is failing I'm not sure we can do anything other than make you comfortable at this point. You have less than one year to live." The scene faded to black and Teresa was staring at Talmadge sobbing. Talmadge was unmoved by her tears, and even less interested in what the doctor had said. He had heard the prognosis before - left in numerous unreturned voice mail messages on his cell phone, emails at work, and even a few text messages. He had also heard the same prognosis from his own doctor about one month ago. Each time he failed to acknowledge his role in Teresa's and his illness. He looked back at Teresa with contempt in his eyes and asked, "Why should I care about your problems?"

Teresa wiped her tear stained face with a silk scarf she removed from her Coach purse and regained her composure. She even managed to push out a smile while she spoke. "My problem, is that what you think this is...my problem? I see you need a refresher." She rose to her feet and stood directly above Talmadge looking down at him as if daring him to even think about looking back. She began telling her story, their story and Talmadge was forced to listen.

"I was happy before I met you. I was in love with Anthony, a wonderful man who loved me back. In some regards he loved me more than I loved myself. Sure we were having some problems and in hindsight I now know I was the one who was having the most problems. I was trying to adjust to the pressures of my new job as an Associate Principal at an elementary school; a guy who was stalking her had recently killed my best friend. On top of that Anthony had just told me he was thinking about looking for another job out of state. With all of that going on it was hard for me to see how happy, and fortunate I really was at the time. I was in love and struggling trying to decide to end my relationship with Anthony, or to hold on and work things out. How I wish I had made better choices, but you know what they say hindsight is 20/20. If I had been left to my own devices I probably would have made better choices, but instead I allowed you to come into my life and convince me otherwise."

"I never even gave you my phone number, yet one day out of the blue you called me. It would be some time later before I found out that you actually got my number from Anthony, the love of my life and your fraternity brother. He borrowed your cell phone one day and called me and you saved the number plotting your future use of it. You waited until one day you knew he was out of town and you called me. At first I tried not to talk to you, but I was flattered by your Charm and persistence. It all seemed so innocent in the beginning you're good I will give you that. You positioned yourself to be my friend and confidant. You were someone who was going to help me understand Anthony. You told me how lucky you thought he was to have me, and you only wanted to help me stay with him. Like a fool I shared my personal life and problems with you. You and I talked on the telephone and began meeting for drinks. I had surgery and you brought me flowers and cookies. When I was well we even met for a lunch and dinner a couple of times. Neither of us ever mentioned this to Anthony, but he became suspicious."

"When he questioned me about spending time with someone else I lied to him. Never saying a word about my spending time with you. After all you and I were just friends. I had no intention of getting involved with you in a romantic manner. You were married, I knew your reputation for being a jerk, - and you were fat. Still with all of that you managed to display character traits that were similar to my Anthony. You both even have the same Zodiac sign. There were things I saw in you that I used to see in Anthony, unfortunately, the stress of trying to balance his professional career with his ex-wife's demands on his time had begun to eat at him."

"I should have helped him get through his rough times instead I held his situation against him. Then one night outside of this very bar you kissed me. A line was crossed, and neither of us thought enough of Anthony to tell him. When he found out and he was devastated. Somehow he found a way to access both of our cell phone records, and saw that you and I were talking on the telephone everyday two and three times a day. I began calling you more than I was calling him. He even saw that I had called you on the fourth of July at 4 o'clock in the morning repeatedly until you called me back. When he confronted me with the telephone bill I lied about it. Eventually I confessed to everything. I told him how you said that you loved me. After all that is what you told me right Talmadge? Anthony even asked you about your interest in me and you lied. If you loved me why didn't you just tell him? Why didn't you tell your wife?" Talmadge remained silent.

Looking away from Talmadge Teresa continued with her tale. "Never mind you don't have to answer those questions. I already know the answers, I just found them too late." Teresa turned and began pointing her finger at Talmadge's forehead. Talmadge did not move he sat there lifeless listening as Teresa recalled their meetings and dealings. His body was motionless but his brain was moving at light speed. He too was processing his meeting Teresa and his involvement with her. He was also contemplating his interactions with Anthony his fraternity brother and Teresa's boyfriend at the time. Oddly he never gave any thought to his own wife Nancy and their two children.

A sinister grin crawled from the corners of his face and made it's way to the center of his mouth as he continued to remember the details. He had wanted Teresa from the first day he saw her with Anthony. To him it mattered not that she was dating his fraternity brother, she was just another material object that Talmadge wanted to possess. She was a trophy, a test, if he could add her to his collection he would truly be the big man mentally that he had become physically. Teresa was right Talmadge had waited for just the right moment when he sensed a weakness in order to make his move. He had stolen her phone number and saved it in his cell phone without Anthony ever knowing. He had told her that he loved her knowing full well that he didn't mean a single word of it. He knew that would help him gain her trust, she was vulnerable and would fall for it. He had done everything according to his own sinister plan and the grin now residing on his face said he had no regrets for his schemes and manipulations. All of these thoughts and more came to him in one second and continued to dance around his ever-swelling head all while Teresa was pouring her heart out to him.

"One of the saddest truths I have had to face is that even after I hurt Anthony and changed his life, he still tried to warn me about you. He told me that I was not the only woman you were cheating on your wife with, and that you couldn't possibly love me. I thought he was just being the typical scorned lover - player-hater, trying to put you down for your having stolen me from him. I was wrong, only time would prove how wrong I was. Dead wrong!"

"Sure I enjoyed the money you spent on me. The time we spent traveling to Rockford, St. Louis, your conversation and even the physical part of the sex we had, it filled a void, I was suffering from low self-esteem back then and your compliments and fun-loving spirit lifted my self-esteem temporarily. I felt guilty for allowing you to get so close to me, and I let that guilt keep you close to me. The truth is I ran off the only man who ever loved me for me to be with a fake, fat, good for nothing coward like you. At first I ignored the symptoms of my illness. I kept hoping I would get better. I kept getting more and more sick. I had never been sick like this before sleeping with you, and eventually due in part to my illness, but more because of your shallowness I pulled away from you as well. Once I stopped sleeping with you, you stopped hanging out with me. No more phone calls, no more cookies, no text messages, nothing. It became apparent that a great number of people knew about us even though you were married. Your friends and fraternity brothers always knew when we were together, and I soon learned that I had a new reputation among them. I had gone from Anthony's woman to Talmadge's whore. I was labeled just another one of your mistresses. My sudden and dramatic weight loss was the last straw. People at work thought I was some sort of drug addict the weight loss was so sudden. Even my doctor was immediately alarmed when I went to see him. He was so alarmed he convinced me to take an H.I.V. test, the results of which you just relived with me."

"To add insult to injury you were the first person I reached out to and you had the nerve then to suggest just as you have done now that I somehow contracted this disease on my own, that you had nothing to do with it. It was a difficult time for me, I had to notify past lovers that they needed to get tested. Some were very upset but all of them including Anthony did the responsible thing and got tested. You were the only one to avoid your responsibility. Fortunately, my list of lovers over the past years was limited to five people including you. The four others all tested negative for H.I.V. I was given a complete blood work-up before I had my surgery. That was before I began seeing you. I was perfectly healthy then. I contracted the disease after my surgery, once I started seeing you. You gave it to me. You gave me this death sentence, and then tried to blame me you selfish bastard!"

"Imagine how embarrassed I was to have to list your name as the only person I had slept with in the past two years while simultaneously realizing that you had been sleeping with every woman around including your wife." Tears flowed down her face as she continued to speak, images that coincided with her words were shown in the blackness behind her forcing Talmadge to relive every devastating experience she described. Talmadge became visibly disturbed again as he rose from the booth it disappeared. A solid blackness enveloped them both. Talmadge looked at Teresa and shook his head.

"You are sick, I didn't give you any disease! This is crazy! I want to leave. Get away from me right now- you are sick!!!"

Teresa turned her back to him, and shouted "Leave, you haven't seen enough yet. You have not seen how this ends." Suddenly there was a rush of light and Talmadge and Teresa were transported to a hospital room. In the center of the room was a pale and sickly Teresa lay motionless in bed. Tubes were extending from her body, monitors and other equipment hummed and beeped as a slim dark figure entered the room. He was not a doctor; this figure was dressed in a business suit, not a lab coat and was carrying two-dozen red roses and a bag of red 'Twizzlers'. He approached the bed and bent down to kiss Teresa on the forehead. "You came," she said in a voice that was barely audible over the beeps and blips of the hospital machinery. "I never thought you would talk to me again," she whispered.

"You still mean a great deal to me." The man replied. "I feel so sorry for you, you don't deserve to be here," he continued as he sat the roses on the nightstand next to the hospital bed. He opened the 'Twizzlers' and sat on the edge of the bed close to Teresa. "I brought you something," he said handing Teresa a 'Twizzler'.

She lifted her left arm to accept the candy almost disconnecting the I.V. from her tiny hand. "Thanks" she said a weak smile trying to grow on her face. It was a painful smile, but she found pleasure in it. A solitary teardrop fell from her face and then as if leading a parade a continuous line of teardrops followed the first one down Teresa's face and onto the hospital gown she was wearing. They were both silent, the well dressed man in the business suit reached out and held Teresa's left hand with his left hand and wiped her tears with his right hand.

A nurse entered the room to check Teresa's chart, and change the fluid in the I.V. bottle. The nurse smiled at the man, and then realizing that she had interrupted a special moment departed with a polite head nod. Her face still wet with tears

Teresa used all of her remaining strength to position herself to sit up so she could look the man in the eye. "I am so sorry for treating you so bad," Teresa said.

"Teresa, this is not the time nor the place" the man replied patting her left hand with his right. He began to squeeze her hand a little tighter "That's in the past, the most important thing is that I am here now, I have forgiven you, and everything will be alright". Teresa exhaled a sigh of relief, and the two of them sat talking for hours. Both trying to update the other on the three years they had spent apart since their break-up. Anyone witnessing the scene would never have known the two were anything other than the closest of friends or the most intimate of lovers. Their body language and chemistry seemed so in synch that it could only have been garnered from a lifetime of shared intimate moments, their constant eye contact signaling the deepest emotions for each other.

Teresa had not had too many visitors since she had become hospitalized. A few co-workers had stopped by, but most people were unaware of her ailment. A.I.D.S was the type of disease that robbed its victims of the niceties that came with other ailments. Teresa was a typical victim in that regard, she was ashamed to share her illness with those close to her. She did not want to answer questions about her lifestyle. She didn't like what having this illness implied to others. She was young, intelligent, well educated, and gainfully employed. She had just purchased her dream house and was driving a brand new BMW

735i. How could someone like her end up with this disease?

None of those material items mattered to her at that moment. Somehow this one visitor had brought a level of pleasure to her that she had honestly not known since their break-up. As the evening wore on she thought about how she had abused Anthony's trust, and turned her back on him and their relationship. Now he was here in her time of need. "He had always been there for her," she thought. With her strength fading Teresa attempted to raise her head again to speak. The words seemed to be stuck in her throat. Her lips parted as she whispered his name. Anthony leaned in close and looked her in the eye. He could feel her grip on his hand loosening. A tear fell from his face as he kissed her lips softly.

Teresa had passed away. In her fading moments she was never able to muster up enough strength to say, "Anthony I love you", although she had tried. Instinctively Anthony knew what she was trying to do and whispered out his own "I love you too" as he placed her hand back on the bed and tried to ease himself out of the way of the nurses and doctors who had rushed into the room responding to the whistles and alarms raised by the various machines and monitoring devices that Teresa was connected to.

The hospital room disappeared, and once again Talmadge and Teresa were enveloped in blackness. Teresa stood with her back to Talmadge hands covering her face devastated by the image of her own death at Anthony's side. After a brief and uncomfortable silence Teresa spoke, hands still covering her face but her words very clear." You never once acknowledged my illness. You never came to visit me in the hospital. I called you, left you messages, but nothing. You didn't even have the decency to attend my funeral. After all that you have put me through and all that you have witnessed here today you still have the nerve to stand here and pretend as if you have done nothing wrong. I know you are not sorry for what you did to me, but you are sorry. You are a sorry excuse for a human being. You are a sorry excuse for a male. You don't even rate being called a man. You are just a male. I am sorry for you. Regardless of how you feel about me I still feel sorry for you. You just don't get it."

Having had her say Teresa walked into the darkness, never once looking back at Talmadge again. She simply disappeared.

"A.D."

Screw you!" Talmadge screamed into the darkness looking in the direction Teresa had gone, his empty words cascading through the air and echoing throughout the darkness. He looked and waited hoping Teresa would reappear, that she would yell something back confirming that he was not alone. No such confirmation came. "That's right go on leave me here, just like I left you. You were nothing to me but a quick screw - another notch on Chuckee Poo's belt. Screw you and that hand holding, punk boyfriend of yours." Talmadge looked at his watch again. The time remained unchanged. He was unraveling and he knew it. He was unsure of how much more of this he could take. "None of this is real, I am going to wake up with one heck of a hangover in the morning. I am going to wake up!" Talmadge tried to convince himself.

Clap, clap, clap..."Very good Mr. Green, very good!" called a loud masculine voice from the darkness.

"Who said that?" screamed Talmadge as he whirled his gargantuan mass of flesh around searching in the distance for a body to match the voice he had heard. "Show yourself!" Talmadge demanded.

"You are always trying to boss somebody around. It didn't work then and it sure as hell is not going to work now Mr. Green". The words seemed to come from every direction.

Talmadge squeezed his eyes tightly trying to scan the dark for any sign of life. "I need a drink," he thought, his hands twitching - longing for a bottle to hold.

"Yeah I know how you feel I'd like to have a nice cold one myself." The voice taunted Talmadge from the safety of the dark. The unseen communicator made Talmadge feel more enraged. It gave him a very eerie feeling not to be in control of the situation. It bothered him immensely not knowing who or what his adversary was. His education, his career, his relationships all were tightly monitored and controlled by him. Now here he was in a strange place having strange experiences taunted by a strange voice. All of this after having faced people from his past, and now he was afraid of what was coming next. "Show yourself. You're a tough guy in your little hiding place. Why don't you show yourself?" Talmadge was still yelling trying to coax the voice into showing itself.

Talmadge cracked his knuckles and continued to scan the darkness for any signs of life. Everywhere that Talmadge turned the darkness disappeared replaced with walls, and floors until finally Talmadge Green stood in a fully enclosed room. The sign on the wall read "Sunnyside Community Center". A door at the end of the room crept open and in walked a young black man. He was impeccably dressed and well groomed. His tapered haircut peeked out from under his wool hat and faded into his freshly shaved beard and connecting mustache. His attire was a who's who of modern fashion design. His Shoes were Johnston and Murphy brown eel skin. His slacks were Chocolate brown wool baggies from Perry Ellis complete with cuffs and pleats. His shirt was a plain white button-down covered by a burnt orange sweater vest with a three-button front. The opening in the vest was wide and long enough to expose the brown, orange, and crème colored Van Heusen silk tie. A crème and brown colored blazer added a classic look to the ensemble, which was topped off by the crème and brown wool hat. He looked as if he could have easily been mistaken for rappers 'Common' or 'Mos Def' if they were on their way to an awards show. In any event the man was sharp, he walked with a confidence that said, "The world is mine".

He entered the room as if he were the guest of honor at his own coronation. He circled Talmadge sizing him up as much as he was allowing Talmadge to examine him. He stared at Talmadge from top to bottom making careful note of his obesity through a few facial gestures. Shaking of his head here, a smirk and a giggle there, all done in order to belittle the behemoth of a man Talmadge had grown into. In some ways he was belittling Talmadge with his glare in other ways he pitied him. He accomplished both without ever saying a word.

Talmadge was nervous sweat ran from his pores as if someone had shot off a starters pistol. Talmadge had never allowed another man to intimidate him at least not since his childhood. However, this young, dapper dressed black man was full of confidence and the way he convincingly displayed it made

Talmadge all the more uncomfortable.

"You nervous ain't you?" the young man said. "I can smell the fear coming off of you - or is that bacon grease oozing out of your pores?" he said laughing as he now stood directly in front of Talmadge making a frown as if the smell of Talmadge was forcing his nostrils to contort. He stood directly in front of Talmadge staring him square in the eye. Even though he was a few inches shorter than Talmadge, and weighing considerably less than him as well, he was somehow the bigger man. He extended his hand. Talmadge was startled and immediately jumped back, the rolls in his stomach continuing to move even after Talmadge was standing still. "Adrian Williams is my name but you can call me A.D. since we are old friends and all" the young man said waiting for Talmadge to shake his hand.

Talmadge regained his composure refusing to accept the young mans gesture. He turned a cold shoulder to him as he uttered the following "I don't believe I know you sir". Withdrawing his hand the man who asked to be called A.D. laughed aloud and replied, "You really don't recognize me do you? It's only been about five years since the last time we saw one another. I thought meeting you here at Sunnyside would help you remember me. I am a little disappointed. Five years ago I was a 16-year-old high school student. Some people would say I was a troubled youth - I prefer to think of myself at that time as a kid at a crossroad. I had been coming to this very community center everyday for two years before you showed up. I came here because it was safe. It was a place where I could express myself, through my words. I wrote poems and rhymes that told the stories I witnessed everyday in the streets growing up in Chicago. The wild 100's are what some people called this community, but I called it my inspiration.

Talmadge re-examined A.D., this time with a great deal more interest, "I remember you now, but you can't be that kid" Talmadge stated, asking the question as much as he was stating it as fact. No sooner had the word "kid" escaped from his mouth had A.D. jumped on Talmadge, the silver barrel of the Smith and Wesson nine millimeter pistol pressed deep into Talmadge's chest. "Don't you ever call me a kid again! I told you my name is A. D. - not kid, not boy or chum, not little man none of that, my name is A. mother-f-ing D. but as I said earlier you can call me A.D." He slid the hammer back with his thumb. The smooth click of the trigger locking itself into its firing position resonated as loud as any of the words A.D. had uttered. "You got that fat boy?" he added as he slapped Talmadge on his right cheek three times lightly.

If it weren't for the huge amount of fat that made up his chest Talmadge's heartbeat would have been felt in A.D.'s hand as he held the barrel of the pistol against Talmadge. But the walls of fat which made up Coleman Talmadge Green created their own sound barrier shielding Talmadge from the embarrassment of A.D. knowing how truly afraid he was at that point. With beads of sweat jumping off of his forehead

Talmadge managed to will himself to nod his head up and down indicating his understanding of his nearly fatal mistake. "I'm sorry," he said. "I didn't mean to be disrespectful, I mean I was not trying to be disrespectful. It's just that you look older than 21.

"Your fat behind looks older than 43 too but what's that got to do with the price of tea in China? Now all of the sudden you are concerned about my age", replied an angered A.D. He stepped back a few feet, away from Talmadge but kept the gun pointed at him until he was more than arms length away. In five years life in the city had robbed him of his youth. He had grown up fast and hard during those five years. He had put down his pen and picked up a pistol. He had traded in the safety and refuge of the community center for the respect and profit of the streets. He could easily pass for age 30 at first glance.

"I'm going to put this away now, I hope I won't have to pull it back out again." A.D. slipped the gun back into its special place amid the designer clothes he was wearing with the symbolic precision of a Samurai warrior sheathing his Katana sword. Suddenly the room filled with teenage boys and girls. An apparently youthful A.D. was at the front of the room with a notebook in his hand. He looked at the audience and began to recite:

> *I'm A Poet*
> *When I speak from my heart*
> *I have to be careful*
> *Don't worry I'm not fearful*
> *It's just some hear my words and*

think "oh this brother is weak".
All the time I know the truth,
my words are just too deep.
I'm a Poet.

I give words life as easily as
Judges give it to brothers.
Push them out of my head onto paper
with the pride and the pain of a
delivering mother.
With a pen in hand my words take flight.
Launching freedom with each stroke that I
write.
I'm a poet.

My words analyze, tell stories, and inspire
dreams.
From the deeply political, the subtly erotic
to the way straight up obscene.
I write with such color that you feel my
images too.
You don't hear my words you see what I
want you to.
I'm a poet.
Roses are and violets are blue.
Blue like the Caribbean Sea on a calm day.
Day and night become lost when we are
together.
Together like a left shoe and a right...
Right by my side is where I need my love,
Love yourself, your community, and your
people.

People have died so that you can be.
Beware of the pitfalls of greed and jealousy.
Jealousy kills more people than war ever has.
Has everyone lost their common sense?
Since I now have your attention
did I forget to mention?
I'm a poet.

Don't mess with me my writing knows no equal.
My thoughts so deep swimming in them should be illegal.
It's proven fatal to some when my words go over their head.
Forget the original or the remake
My words capture the stories of the living dead.
A Black nation asleep,
once awakened can't be beat.
There will be no repeat,
No surrender, or retreat.
Complete freedom period,
this or death and defeat
if again you ever think to mistreat,
enslave, abuse, cheat,
The original people oh so unique
without who's knowledge and labor you could not complete,
a sentence,
a mathematical equation,
circumnavigation,

irrigation,

crop rotation,

Construction of the greatest capitalist and
hypocritical, democratic nation.

You better pray for salvation,
from my metaphorical retaliation.
All this because you couldn't see me
feel me or
even know it.
I'll say it for the last time...
I'm a poet.

The kids at the community center stood, and cheered as
A.D. walked off the makeshift stage. He was greeted with high-
fives and shoulder pats. One girl, Amber even kissed him on the
cheek, which caught the young poet off guard making him blush.
Everyone in the center approved of A.D. and his gift with words
except for two people who stood in the back of the room. A
younger and slightly thinner Talmadge was standing next to him
a white teenage boy named Rich Dillingham. Rich was a short
red-haired white kid with a head that was disproportionately
larger than his body making him look like a living-breathing
"bobble-head" doll. He was 16 years old with a face full of
freckles but his lack of height made him look more like a 12 year
old than a teenager. He was one of the few White kids who still
lived in the neighborhood and once Talmadge Green became a
volunteer Rich felt as if he could get away with whatever he
wanted.

From the first day Talmadge stepped in the center as a volunteer he had taken an interest in Rich. In the two months that Talmadge had been volunteering he connected with Rich, there bond was so strong that Talmadge had convinced Rich that he should not only attend college but Law school after that. Talmadge liked Rich maybe because he was white, maybe because he shared Talmadge's desire for material possessions, or maybe because he recognized that Rich didn't seem to fit in and was picked on by the black kids just as he had been in his youth. A.D. was no exception when it came to picking on Rich. A.D. had a resentment of Whites and often wrote about the "White man and his plot to destroy the black man" in his poetry and raps. Always making sure to deliver his lyrics with a death defying glare fixed on Rich. Talmadge remembered his own adolescence. He too was often picked on by the black kids and felt powerless to do anything about it. In Rich he saw himself young, ambitious and constantly misunderstood by all of those around him.

As a volunteer at the Sunnyside community center after school program Talmadge made sure that Rich always got his way. No matter what the situation Talmadge always made sure Rich never got in trouble for his behavior. Rich knew he had a guardian in Talmadge, and took full advantage of it whenever Talmadge was around. Today would be no exception, as A.D. left the stage and returned to his place in the audience of teenagers, Rich greeted him with the universally understood flipping of his middle finger. A.D. unphased by Rich's gesture continued toward his seat making a mental note of the white boys actions.

Jealous of the attention and accolades A.D. was receiving for his latest poetic masterpiece Rich decided to turn up the pressure between he and A.D. Rich walked over to A.D. and snatched A.D.'s notebook from his hand. Before A.D. could react Rich was running full steam towards the opposite end of the community center. Rich turned laughing and taunting A.D. with his own notebook. "Is this the crap you just read?" he said holding the notebook open by the spiral. By now the 16-year old A.D. was demanding the return of his notebook promising Rich that he would be willing to forgive and forget the whole thing if Rich would simply place the notebook back in his hands. The other kids were in a fury all yelling and waiting for A.D. to punish Rich for his disrespect.

Rich looked at Talmadge to see if he was going to intervene. The younger Talmadge gave Rich a twisted grin that on the surface seemed to say, "Go ahead I've got your back". With that gesture of confirmation Rich set in motion a chain of life altering events that would seal his and A.D.'s fate.

'Rrriiippp' went the first page from the notebook. "How do you like that nigga?" Rich screamed while ripping more pages out of A.D.'s notebook. Rich's hands were fixed to rip more pages when the first punch was felt and heard. The young A.D. had punched Rich straight in his nose causing an explosion of blood to emerge. Young A.D. hit him again with an uppercut to the chin. Rich was going down and young A.D. was going down on top of him. He was holding Rich's bloodied t-shirt in his left hand and punching him repeatedly with his right.

In that short instance between his first punch opening Rich's nose and his body hitting the floor young A.D. had unleashed a fury of blows and was now sitting straddled across Rich's chest delivering even more punishment to his already bloodied and swollen face. "I don't care how many black people you live around you bet not ever let me hear you call another black person a Nigga. You don't have that right!" young A.D. lectured while punching Rich some more. Young Talmadge rushed in and grabbed A.D. screaming, "What's wrong with you kid?" He flung young A.D. across the room, placing himself as a barrier between the two youths. Even in his younger days Talmadge's mass was enough of a wall to prevent young A.D. from even seeing Rich let alone reaching him to continue his assault.

"My notebook?" young A.D. yelled, inquiring as to the whereabouts of his notebook, demanding it's return with the same two word utterance.

"That's it I am going to see to it that you are banned from here for good," young Talmadge said while pushing young A.D. toward the front door of the community center. "You are nothing but a little savage," Talmadge continued. The other teens were a buzz with excitement over the fight. Some laughing at

Rich, some worried about A.D., but all agreeing that Rich had gotten exactly what he deserved for crossing the line. He had been warned before about using the infamous "n-word" but he apparently had not learned his lesson. The teens now watched in disbelief as Talmadge unleashed a verbal assault of his own at the 16-year old A.D. Every time A.D. tried to speak Talmadge ordered him to remain silent. He threw words like "useless, and despicable" at A.D. He concluded by promising to have the police come if A.D. did not leave the center at once.

"My notebook" A.D. again pleaded "I just want to get my notebook". Talmadge continued to push the boy out the front door of the community center. A.D. tried to return and retrieve his notebook, but there was no getting through Talmadge. There was no way of getting around him either. Talmadge's frame occupied the entire width of the doorway. A.D. could barely see past him, and he knew he would never be able to squeeze through the narrow opening as long as Talmadge stood there.

Reg was another kid who at one time was a regular at Sunnyside. He now only showed up once every blue moon to recruit more kids for gang membership or to listen to A.D. perform. Most days he was too busy selling drugs and hanging with his fellow Black Gangster Disciples to stop by the center. He had seen the entire exchange between A.D. and Rich. Reg was slowly approaching Rich who was still sitting in the middle of the floor where A.D. had left him. Reg picked up A.D.'s notebook from the floor and tucked it under his arm. He then punched Rich in the face causing him to scream out in agony and made the other teens roar with laughter. Reg yelled out "G.D." while displaying a hand-signal that resembled a pitchfork with his right hand, and held A.D.'s notebook in his left showing his friend he now had possession of the prized notebook. Laughing he ran out the back door of the community center signaling for A.D. to meet him around the back. The two of them disappearing into the neighborhood laughing and recounting the fight. The entire scene faded into nothingness, and Talmadge was alone with the 21-year old A.D. again.

"It's eerie ain't it Nigga?" A.D. asked sarcastically. "I mean watching yourself like that - seeing how you was back then"

Talmadge was visibly disturbed he had seen so much. He badly wanted and needed a drink. Looking at his watch again he thought, "I'm going to be late" even though not one second had ticked off of the watch.

"Dude you still don't get it, do you? You ain't going to be late. You are already too late- it's over fat boy you might as well start singing because you are the closest thing we have to a fat lady around here - ha, ha, ha. Face it it's over, finished, game and match - that's tennis talk, but I bet your fat butt never played tennis much did you?"

Talmadge spun around facing A.D. and stepped toward him, his eyes flashing red with anger. A.D. simply pulled his jacket to the left revealing the butt of the nine millimeter pistol shaking his head and hand at Talmadge he warned "I don't think you want to do that now do you?" Talmadge froze in his tracks. He put his head down in shame, hung his shoulders low and began to turn back around. Suddenly, he spun around with the speed and grace of a killer whale lashing out in the direction where A.D. had stood. It was too late A.D. was gone. Talmadge was alone in complete darkness again. "You just have not learned fat boy" A.D.'s fading voice called through the darkness. Don't worry I am sure we will see each other again - soon".

The Thin Man

The darkness and silence dwarfed Talmadge. It was as if he were standing in a huge empty warehouse with no lights. He looked to his left and then to his right repeatedly. It did not matter which way he looked direction had no meaning when one is surrounded by such overwhelming darkness, that's how complete it was. The silence was deafening to Talmadge. He kept looking for people to reappear, Carlos Hosey, the cleaning woman, Teresa, A.D. - anyone. His mind kept searching for alcohol. He could see the small glass filled to the rim with Crown Royal and ice. His tongue became salivated with the tingle of liquid anticipation from just the thought of having one small sip. His heart was racing, and his hands sweated profusely. " I am losing my mind" Talmadge thought. Talmadge bellowed, "Who's next? You can't break me! This is all just smoke and mirrors". Talmadge fell backwards onto the darkness and began to laugh aloud. The image was reminiscent of what Santa Clause would look like at a Dave Chapelle show. He would be laughing, and his belly jumping and rolling uncontrollably with each exhalation. A stream of tears washed over Talmadge's face as his laughter changed to sobs. "Why is this happening to me?" he shouted into the darkness.

"It's not happening to you, but because of you" a voice chimed from the darkness. Talmadge rolled over onto his hands and knees. His head rose into a startled state of alertness that mirrored that of elephants when approached by impending danger.

"Who are you?" Talmadge asked still unable to see anyone else in the darkness. Just then a slim figure stepped out of the darkness revealing only his silhouetted outline. "Why I am that who knows you better than you know yourself, but that is not the real answer that you seek is it Talmadge?" The figure spoke with the relative calm of an angel. His tone when he spoke demonstrated that he was a man without a single concern in this world. Talmadge was also no longer afraid. He lifted himself from the floor and stood erect again. A chair appeared out of nowhere, and Talmadge instinctively sat down patiently waiting for the shadowy figure to expose him self. The thin man remained in the shadows. "What questions do you really have Coleman Talmadge Green?" the figure asked politely. "I will answer all of your questions as best I can" The thin man stated without a hint of emotion in his voice.

"Who are you?" Talmadge asked not wanting to waste any more time or give the thin man reason to go back on his word. "I have already answered that question, I simply am that who knows you better than you know yourself" replied the thin man. "If you still want to know my name after asking all of your other questions I will give it to you. Now please ask the other questions that you have, you know the ones that are truly pressing". As the thin man completed his sentence a table appeared in front of Talmadge and a hanging light fixture appeared above the table. It was an ordinary table, the kind you would buy to play cards at or bring out for the kids to sit at during large family gatherings. The light hung mysteriously above the table, it's cord disappearing into the darkness. The whole scene looked like an interrogation room from an old black and white movie. Another chair appeared and the thin man slid his slender frame into it and was now seated across from Talmadge. The thin man was still covered in shadows, but Talmadge could see that the thin man was wearing a very expensive three-piece suit. The thin man clasped his hands in front of him atop the card table revealing a Movado wristwatch, a platinum, gold, and diamond encrusted wedding band similar to the one Talmadge himself had once looked at as an anniversary present. The thin man also wore an expensive set of cuff links - gold with a pearl inlay; the white shirtsleeves they were set in had a very crisp freshly dry-cleaned starch and stiffness to it. Talmadge smiled as he thought, "he can't be too bad, he's dressed too nice".

"Okay, how about telling me where I am?" Talmadge asked doubtful that he would receive a truthful answer. "You are in a place called the anti-chamber, think of it as a lobby filled with souls, all waiting for their turn at judgment. "The thin man replied. Talmadge was shocked he sat straight up in his chair and placed his hands on the table. "What do you mean souls waiting for judgment?" Talmadge asked nervously. The thin mans demeanor did not change as he continued to converse with Talmadge. In fact, except for his lips moving he was motionless as he delivered Talmadge the explanation he both wanted and feared. "You my dear Coleman Talmadge Green are dead".

"Dead?" Talmadge interjected.

The thin man motioned with his right hand for Talmadge to stop talking "Wait please allow me to answer your question completely before interrupting me. I assure you all of your questions will be answered. We have plenty of time". Having quieted Talmadge the thin man again clasped his hands in front of him atop the table and continued to speak. "Everyone who dies must come to this place, at least their souls must come here. Your body was destroyed in the car accident. This is your soul that is seated here before me. Everything that you used your time on Earth to become is represented by the soul that sits here now". The thin man paused and a mirror appeared in front of Talmadge completely blocking his view of the thin man. "This is what your soul looks like" he said.

Talmadge looked in the mirror and was relieved to see a very familiar sight. He saw his huge mass of a body dressed for work looking exactly as he had looked when he left home this morning. He smiled. The mirror vanished as suddenly as it had appeared and the thin man began to speak again. "Every soul must come here and wait. It is here where the soul must meet with five other souls it has come into contact with while living on Earth. Some of the five died before the soul who is waiting others die after. In either case your soul waits here until it meets with the other five souls".

"Why do I have to meet them?" Talmadge asked impatiently, hoping that he had not interrupted the thin man again. "Life and death exist in 360 degrees, a full circle. What goes around must come back around in order for the cycle to be complete. This is one of the main laws of universal truth and justice, commonly referred to as karma. You must come here and face that which you have had a role in creating before you can begin anew as a spiritual being. It is the universes way of providing closure," the thin man explained.

"Oh really" asked Talmadge in somewhat disbelief. He sat quiet for a moment trying to absorb all that he had heard. Once he gathered his thoughts he presented the thin man with his next question. "If all that you are saying is true why did I have to meet with those four people? I mean Teresa I might understand - I really knew her. The rest of those people I barely even knew their names. As a matter of fact I still don't remember the cleaning ladies name. I don't need any closure with her; I can't even remember her name. I don't know her."

The thin man was no longer seated across from Talmadge he was now standing behind him. He leaned over and whispered into Talmadge's ear "Do you really believe that you had no part in creating the soul that these people now posses? If so, I truly feel sorry for you". Not seeing the thin man across from him was one thing, but hearing him whispering in his ear, feeling his hot breath on the back of his neck and never seeing him actually move was something altogether different. Talmadge barely had time to be afraid before the thin man reappeared in his chair sitting directly across from Talmadge hands clasped together on the table as if he had never left his seat. His face was still hidden in the shadows.

"Look! I just want to move on with my life, or my death, or whatever it is you call it," Talmadge exclaimed sweat jumping off his forehead as if it were beads of water dropping into grease filled skillet. "I'm afraid it is going to take more than you just wanting to move on, you have to complete the circle", the thin man stated calmly.

"Okay then lets complete the circle then" Talmadge demanded.

"As you wish, we shall start with him then". The thin man waved his right hand and the surroundings were instantly filled with images of Carlos Hosey. In some of the images Carlos was a young college student, in others he was a young Marine. There were even some images of him as the disfigured soul Talmadge had met.

"When you met Mr. Hosey he was full of promise and ambition. He wanted to be an accountant just like you. Despite his easygoing personality you disliked him from the start". The thin man began painting a history with words.

"I never really disliked him," Talmadge said quite defensively. "Mr. Green I caution you, this is a place of universal truth and justice. Your lies will find no refuge here", the thin man countered. With that Talmadge eased his huge frame back into a more relaxed posture in the chair, remaining silent waiting for the thin man to continue with his debriefing. "You held the one thing that Carlos Hosey could not control against him, his race. You despised him because he was black. He never had a chance with you, simply because he was black. You used every opportunity that presented itself to sabotage him in your class. The images of Talmadge and Carlos during their group project meetings began to flash by. "Your efforts to assault his character resulted in him failing the introductory accounting course which in turn got him kicked out of the accounting department. Once that happened his father refused to pay for him to return to school so he joined the Marine Corp".

"I didn't make him join the Marines" Talmadge interjected.

"You created the circumstances which forced him to enlist. Had he been left alone to succeed in the class, and the major Carlos Hosey would have become a successful accountant. Your campaign against him and his academic abilities was successful and had far reaching consequences that you Mr. Green must come to terms with in order for you to move on". The thin man leaned back in his chair and now his entire torso was submerged in darkness. The scene again resembled an old black and white gangster movie where the good guys shine a bright light in the face of the bad guy giving him just enough information to make him sweat. Talmadge was indeed sweating. Sitting under the intense light under the calm scrutiny of the thin man Talmadge had to acknowledge that he had in deed set out to intentionally ruin Carlos Hosey. His words came out and at first were barely audible. "I just wanted his black ass out of my group. I never thought he would have to quit school," Talmadge whispered. His volume increasing he continued, "Sure I knew if he failed the class he would have to change majors, but I didn't want to compete with a black guy for top honors or internships, in the accounting department". Suddenly Carlos Hosey's soul appeared standing next to the thin man. He had on his dress blue Marine uniform and was smiling. His face was no longer disfigured and he was a complete young man again.

"Thank you Cheese old boy. You don't know how happy I am to hear you admit what you did to me. For years I doubted myself. I wondered if I had actually been the type of poor student you had made me out to be. I even began to hate being black because of you. I never knew for sure what happened to me or why until just now. Now I can move on, I am whole once again. I just needed to hear you own up to what you did to me. Coleman Talmadge Green - I forgive you and I hope that one day you will complete your own circle". With those last words Carlos Hosey's soul faded into nothingness leaving Talmadge and the thin man in utter darkness again. Talmadge was the first to break the silence by asking "Now what? Am I free to move on now?" There was no remorse in his voice, no semblance of sorrow for the life he had altered. The thin man shook his head in the shadows, and coldly answered Talmadge with a resounding "No". It was the first time the thin mans vocal tone had reflected anything other than calm. "We have another person to see," he said. Once again he waved his hand, and the space was filled with images of an elderly black woman. Scenes of her at home with a young black man, scenes of her at work cleaning offices, were being shown simultaneously. There were even images of her sitting in Mr. Weis's office.

"Her name was Glenda Jean Spencer and she cleaned your office at Arthur Anderson for a living. She had worked at that company for ten years prior to your coming. She would have been eligible for retirement this year had she not lost her job" the thin man began.

"And I guess you are going to say that is my fault as well? Talmadge asked changing his tone to match the coldness he sensed in the thin man's voice.

"Talmadge I am only answering your questions. The truth simply is what it is. Weren't you the one who was drinking in your cubicle and other places at work?" Suddenly the images of Glenda Jean were gone replaced with images of Talmadge at work consuming alcohol. The images were crystal clear as if being displayed on a high definition plasma screen television, only these images were shown in mid-air. "Glenda Jean Spencer was raising her grandson, and took the position with Arthur Anderson because of the tuition reimbursement program for employees and their dependents. She wanted her grandson to attend the best college and knew that working for Arthur Anderson would guarantee her being able to afford it. He was set to begin classes at Northwestern University in Evanston, Illinois in the fall, but you changed that as well. You lied on her just as you had lied on Carlos, only this time you did it out of desperation. You had to blame your drinking on someone, or you would have been discovered". The images of Talmadge drinking seemed to be replaying themselves over and over again. The truth is Talmadge had been drinking increasingly at work for the past year and a half, and each of these scenes were now replaying every drink he had taken.

Talmadge again protested, "I never thought she would get fired for drinking. She's just the cleaning lady my God. How was I to know they would make a big deal about another low class black woman drinking? What did they expect from a black cleaning lady? I thought they would just suspend her a few days, or maybe send her to a treatment program. I was trying to help the old woman get a few days off work, you know some time off with pay". The thin man rose from his seat across from Talmadge and warned him again "This is a place of universal truth and justice your lies - will - find –no- re-fuge – here!" He made sure to stretch every syllable of each word out hoping to impress upon Talmadge the gravity of his situation. Talmadge resolved to put a smirk on his face, and sit quietly once again.

"The sad irony of this situation is that your word was

also in question and alone would not have been enough to get her fired. It was her attempts at protecting you from being discovered that made your accusations of her so believable. Mrs. Spencer always tried to take your alcohol containers out separately from the rest of the trash. She knew from working here for so long what would happen to you if they discovered that you were drinking in the office. In fact the day you pointed the finger of blame at her she had actually come in early to warn you that your supervisor had been going through your trash and asking her questions about your drinking. They were trying to find evidence against you, evidence that she wanted you to know they would not find because she had been disposing of it for you without your knowledge. She trusted you, a tragic and eventually fatal mistake. They caught her with your empty booze bottles in a separate trash bag trying to dispose of them. When she came in early to warn you Ms. Waters and Mr. Weis were waiting for her. They asked her to tell where she had gotten the alcohol bottles from, and she refused to incriminate anyone else. She protected you by keeping quiet. She refused to say whose cubicles she actually got the bottles from".

Talmadge's mouth dropped. He was truly at a loss for words. He asked himself "What have I done"? As if on cue Glenda Jean Spencer appeared in front of him. She was not in her work uniform as before, this time she was wearing her Sunday goes to meeting clothes. A nice blue dress, with a matching wide brim hat. "No need to beat yourself up none." her soft and serene voice came from under the hat. "You had no idea who I was. I should have done just what was right and tended to my own business. Getting fired did not bother me so much; I was so tired of working anyway. If it were just me I could have stopped working a little while ago, I don't need much. I could have stopped working and gone on to glory to be with my Smitty, that was my husbands' name. Getting fired actually hurt Cedric the most. Cedric was my grandson he used to come to work with me some nights and dreamed of being an accountant so he could have a big office like the ones I cleaned. Cedric was so set on going to Northwestern; my getting fired changed all of that. Once I was fired I lost the tuition benefits. I couldn't find another job, not too many job openings for a 62 year-old with a high school diploma you know. Things got hard after a few months we were evicted. We tried living in shelters and bounced around between relatives as well. We ended up back on the streets in the dead of winter. One night outside in that freezing cold was all that it took for me to get sick. Pneumonia is what the doctor said. These old bones just couldn't fight off the cold like they used to. Cedric took me to the county hospital and stayed by my side until the end". Talmadge could not look at Mrs. Spencer. He had a huge lump in his throat as he forced the words "I'm sorry" up through the blockage.

"Hush child no need for all of that. I's be just fine. God has a way of looking out for his children you know. My passing allowed Cedric to collect on my insurance policy. He is going to

Northwestern anyway, and will have plenty of money left over. You need to be saving that sorrow for yourself. I know the Lord, but I got an awful feeling that you don't". Talmadge looked up hoping to gain some more insight from Mrs. Spencer. She was right he had not put forth any effort to get to know God, and now hoped she would help him. Deep down he was secretly hoping that since she knew Jesus on a personal basis she would be able to introduce him or at least put in a good word on his behalf. But it was too late, he looked up just in time to see the old woman walking away and fading into the distance. She was walking and singing, "I'm going up yonder. I'm going up yonder. I'm going up yonder to be with my lord..."

"Don't fret Talmadge we still have another person to see" spoke the emotionless thin man. "I will warn you again this is a place of universal truth and justice your lies..." Talmadge cut him off "Lies will find no refuge here. I heard you the first two times, I get the picture now". The thin man changed his tone again making it more serious "I'm just making sure you know and understand that there are limits to even my patience. I will tolerate no more of your insolence or interruptions. Is that understood"? The thin man placed his palms down on the table as if he were about to push himself up from the table. Instead he fixed his gaze on Talmadge staring at him from the recesses of the shadows. Talmadge could not see the thin mans eyes but he knew the thin mans gaze was fixed on him. The thin man razed his right hand, and made a gesture inviting the next person to step from the darkness. Talmadge jumped from his chair and tried desperately to turn his head away. It was useless countless images now surrounded him. There was no escaping them. Talmadge grabbed his head and tried to cover his eyes. He did everything he could to try to avoid looking at the images and scenes that now confronted him. He kept his objections quiet; mindful of the warning he had just received and the cold eye that was watching him from the darkness.

The images of Teresa at various stages of her life, and one unforgettable image of her in contrast lying motionless in a hospital bed dying from an illness he gave her all played before Talmadge. Even with his hands covering his head and his eyes closed Talmadge saw the images as clear as day. "Let's talk about Teresa, Talmadge," the thin man chided.

"She was a very attractive professional woman in a serious relationship with one of your fraternity brothers when you first met her. From that very first day you plotted and planned on having her added to your personal collection of concubines. She was just another item, which symbolized status for you. After all not only were you an allegedly happily married man, but you had other women you were seeing at the same time as well. There was Jewell, Ruby, Dianne, Kathy, Sonja, and let's not forget the young lady with the birth defect leaving her with only had half of an arm. Some of them were even married to your other fraternity brothers, but most of them involved in some serious relationship with someone else and none of them aware of how you were just manipulating and using each of them. Each of the married ones all ended up divorced. Each of them confided in you their concerns and fears they had about their husbands because they actually thought you wanted to help them. You earned their trust by feeding them information about their husbands, most of which was false. It was funny how you always seemed to call when their husbands were out of town or hanging out with you. It's the same thing you did with Teresa. You started out just trying to be her friend at least that is what you told her. Once you got her attention you started with the secret meetings and private phone conversations. You used the fact that her boyfriend was applying for jobs out of state to justify your interest in pursuing her. It somehow made you feel better going after her knowing that he might be moving to another state. You even told yourself that he didn't really care about her because he refused to discuss their relationship with you. The truth was that he knew the type of low-down, despicable guy you were so he tried to keep his love life as private as he could. In doing so he hoped to keep his and Teresa's relationship safe from interference, gossip and outside influence. He was wrong nothing could keep her safe from a predator like you".

Talmadge refused to look at the thin man. He stood silently with his back turned towards the thin man He began to look at the images but he was nervous. Talmadge was not only nervous, he was agitated - he was afraid. He didn't know who

91

this thin man was, he hadn't even seen his face, but whoever he was he knew a great deal about Talmadge including information about his extramarital affairs. The thin man knew way more than Coleman Talmadge Green was comfortable with him knowing, and it showed in Talmadge's inability to look the thin man in the face.

"How does he know so much about me?" Talmadge thought to himself.

The thin man continued to recount the details about Talmadge and Teresa. "You called Teresa everyday from March until August when her boyfriend found out about the two of you. He even asked you directly if you were calling Teresa, and you being the coward that you are, you lied and said no. You my dear Talmadge are a real piece of work. You worked overtime on Teresa. You even told her you loved her. In all of your being honest with her there were a few things I guess that just slipped your mind. You never told her about the other women in your life did you? You never told her that you had no intentions on leaving your wife. You were even quite careless with your sex life as far as Teresa and all of the others were concerned. You never used protection and you told each and every one of them they were the only person you were sleeping with. You told them all that you had had a vasectomy so you didn't see a need for using condoms. The thin mans words struck a cord deep inside of Talmadge.

That was it Talmadge could not hold his tongue

anymore. He turned toward the thin man and began a tirade equal to his gigantic size. "Those women all knew I was married. They just wanted me to spend some money on them and I did. I paid for everything that I got from them. If they didn't want me to buy it they should not have been selling it. As for Teresa, she was through with her boyfriend and just hadn't told him yet. Yeah, I might have plotted on her from the start but that's because I knew what type of freak she was. She used to mess around with a guy at Arthur Anderson who works in systems, he told me everything I needed to know to get her interested in me. Once I finally got to meet her I knew I could get anything I wanted from her, it was just going to take some time. As far as my fraternity brother Anthony, there is an old saying that goes all of your friends are not in your fraternity and all of your fraternity brothers are not your friends. That sums up my relationship with him. Anthony was no friend of mine, and I didn't owe him a thing. Besides if you think about it I actually did him a favor by showing him exactly what type of two-timing, shallow, whore he had fallen in love with. I don't even know you so why am I even explaining this to you"? Talmadge shoved the table aside and made a rush in the direction the thin man had been seated. When he reached the shadowy figure he was amazed by what he saw. The thin man was gone; the figure in the shadows stood up from the chair and looked Talmadge in the eye. It was Teresa.

"I believe you were saying something Talmadge". The

thin man was again behind Talmadge whispering in his ear. Talmadge turned to his rear to find the thin man had again vanished. Talmadge reeled towards Teresa with his arms flailing wildly. First up in the air, then back to his side, reaching out but then withdrawing them. Teresa was out of the shadows and in full view of Talmadge. The thin man was now at her side stepping backwards his face still concealed in the darkness.

"Yes Talmadge, I believe you were talking about me," Teresa questioned calmly. The last image Talmadge had of Teresa was that of a sick and dying woman lying in a hospital bed. The Teresa who was standing before him seeking answers was not tired, nor sick, she was full of life. She was every bit as beautiful and healthy as she was the very first time Talmadge had met her. Talmadge paused as he looked at her. He was paralyzed by the woman he saw standing before him. Captivated by her gaze he now found himself compelled by some unknown force to answer her question. "I was talking about you," he whispered in a voice that was as soft as cotton.

"The truth is" he continued, "I never respected you at all. You were just something else I saw and wanted to possess. I didn't care who got hurt in the process as long as I could get what I wanted. I felt as though I always deserved the best and you were the best. It burned me up inside every time I saw you with Anthony. He always got more attention with you on his arm than I ever did with my wife. I wanted that attention; I wanted to have you on my arm. I wanted to possess you for my very own".

Talmadge paused momentarily and then continued, "You made it easy for me. I knew you liked the finer things, I could tell by the way you dressed and carried yourself. I did talk to my friend in systems and found out some of what you liked and I waited for my chance. Two things happened that gave me my opportunity. Anthony got his job interview at Duke University and you had your surgery. You were vulnerable. There was no way you were going to leave Chicago. Your job, your friends, your family, were all here in Chicago and you were not going to give that up and follow a man who had not even asked you to marry him. So I started calling you especially when I knew he was out of town. At first I just listened to you and did some light flirting. Once I saw that you never told him about my calling you I knew I had you, it was just a matter of time. I stepped up my game and did exactly what I had done to my other fraternity brothers wives. I started calling you more making sure never to miss calling you when he was out of town. I even invited him out some nights with me so I could call you, and talk about what kind of guy he was to be out enjoying himself leaving you at home alone."

"After awhile it got to be fun to just tease him without him knowing what was going on. I would call him when he was out of town, and make sure I knew exactly when he was coming back to Chicago. It was perfect and he never suspected a thing. I even called him a few times when I was with you just to show you that he would accept my calls and ignore yours." Talmadge paused and a grin slid across his face as if he was reliving one of his best Christmas mornings. He chuckled aloud and then continued with his compelling tell. "Once you trusted me the rest was easy. A few drinks here, a dinner and a gift there, the next thing I knew you were giving it up. After the first time we had been together, no matter what else happened I knew you and Anthony would never be the same. You would do whatever you had to do to make sure he did not find out how you had betrayed him. Telling you I loved you was just my way of keeping pressure on you, making sure you remained confused. I had at least five other women all over the city while I was pursuing you. It was never just you. I was never thinking of leaving my wife and kids for you."

"Eventually, I started to spend less time with you and moved on to my next possession. A few months passed and you started calling me saying you were sick. I had gotten everything I wanted, Anthony had moved on in part due to finding out about you and I. If you were sick I didn't want anything to do with you. Once you came back from the doctor's office I really was not trying to have anything to do with you. I was not going to get tested I hated what you were suggesting. Do you know what would have happened to me if I had tested positive for H.I.V.?"

"If?" Teresa screamed, "What do you mean if you had tested positive? You are the only person I have been sleeping with since Anthony. I never had any problems or symptoms before you. I was tested before my surgery and everything was fine. That was when I was still with Anthony before you and I ever did anything. One year later I am dying and you have the nerve to stand here and act like you had nothing to do with it." Teresa was in tears.

Once again Talmadge hung his head low. He had tried to ignore Teresa when she was alive. He had denied having intercourse with other women still he could not escape his past. Talmadge fell to his knees in front of Teresa. Holding one hand he looked at her and spoke softly. His voice sounding sweet and sincere like it once did when he was trying to seduce her. "I'm so sorry. I never meant for you to die. I was looking for someone to blame for my misfortune and I took it out on you. The truth is the first time you told me you tested positive for HIV, it scared me. I didn't know what to do. I thought if I ignored you everything would be okay. As if somehow making you go away would make the possibility of me having the disease go away. I could not bring myself to believe that I had H.I.V. and A.I.D.S. and I couldn't deal with not having a clue about which one of the countless numbers of women that I had been with had given it to me. I was too afraid to risk coming to see you in the hospital, because I thought seeing you there I would see myself lying their dying. I also would have felt extremely guilty looking at you knowing it was my fault. I didn't even have the courage to attend your funeral. I wish I had had the feelings for you that Anthony had, but I didn't, and I don't now. I was just using you in the same way that I had used so many others before you. Anthony really loved you and I know I played a role in destroying that love".

Teresa pulled her hand back, and used it to wipe her tears. Her face was now radiant and as Talmadge looked at her with regret she was every bit as beautiful as the day they first met. She looked at him and extended her hand helping him get to his feet. "You aren't the only one who is to blame for what happened with Anthony and me, I messed up a lot of that on my own. I allowed myself to be flattered by your money and your compliments and I alone abused the trust and love that Anthony gave me. I know I will have to answer for that one day just as you have had to answer to me. Goodbye Talmadge, I forgive you". Teresa stepped back into the shadows; her eyes fixed on Talmadge a warm smile beaming from her face. Her frame became a silhouette first, and then disappeared completely. She was gone.

Talmadge watched her until his tears completely obscured his vision making even the shadows become a blur. In between tears and sobs Talmadge saw a figure emerging from the shadows. "Teresa!" he hoped aloud. He had more questions and plenty more things he needed to say to her. He wanted to spend some time making up for the way he had mistreated her, he needed to say and to show her exactly how truly sorry he was. He wiped his face and called out "Teresa, I am glad that you came back", but there was no answer. In the quiet darkness, which existed after Talmadge's call for Teresa, there lingered a dreadful sense of fear and frustration. "Teresa's no longer here" called the all to familiar soft voice of the thin man his face still hidden in the shadows. "You will have to continue to ask me your questions, and we still have others to meet".

Talmadge looked down at his watch. Time still had not moved but he was tired. Talmadge felt like he had spent an entire week awake but according to his watch not one second had passed. Whoever this next person was could wait until Talmadge was more rested. He sat back in the chair across from the thin man. The table looked as if he had never shoved it from its original position. The thin man looked as if he had never moved from his original position. He sat there silent hands clasped in front of him on top of the table with the light from the hanging lamp shining down on the center of the table.

Just as Talmadge took his seat images of his drive to work began to appear all around him. "Not now, I can't take anymore of these pictures, or visits I just want to rest" Talmadge said placing his head down on the table as if he were in kindergarten. The images showed Talmadge drinking and driving, and finally his accident. The thin man looked at Talmadge and said, "You can't rest yet there are still answers waiting for you. Your accident this morning involved you and another man yet you never saw his face. How would you feel if I were to tell you that the accident was entirely of your making?"

Talmadge looked up from the table his curiosity peeked. "I know I was drinking and if you think that clouded my judgment I can't argue with you. This is the one thing I already know can we please move on?" The thin man shook his head in the shadows and replied, "My dear Talmadge you have spent all of this time here but you still have not learned. You are wrong once again. The circumstances, which caused your automobile crash today, were created long ago. Today was just your fate meeting with your destiny." Talmadge looked at the thin man with utter confusion on his face and then asked the question he was not sure he was prepared to hear the answer to. "If my drinking and driving did not cause the accident what did?"

The thin man gave an immediate response, which further confused Talmadge. "Your mistreatment of a young black teenager caused this accident and sealed your fate. Your resentment and abuse of everyone black who has come into your life is ultimately what killed you." Just then a figure appeared in the shadows behind the thin man. Talmadge could not see who it was but there was no mistaking the voice.

"This must really burn you up Mr. Green? No pun intended." The figure walking from the shadows said. As the figure stepped into the light Talmadge was shocked. His thoughts were correct but somehow the young man looked different than before. Adrian Williams walked in and was wearing the exact outfit he had on earlier, but this A.D. was different. His face was younger it was the face of a 21 year-old man. He did not have the years that street life had placed on him as he did earlier when he met Talmadge.

"Today was an unfortunate day for both of us. I knew

when I saw you on I - 57 that we were going to clash. You may have forgotten me but I never forgot you or what you did to me way back then. You ran me out of the only safe place I ever knew and released me into the streets. I made it my business to keep up with you. Once I started making good money in the drug game I hired your accounting firm to help me keep track of it. Of course, I created fictitious companies and even requested that you be my accountant. Does the name SCAN Enterprises mean anything to you? You are looking at Mr. SCAN, - tah dah. I even bought a house in your neighborhood, shopped at the same stores as you and you never even noticed me. I admired you when you first started volunteering at the center but you were too busy helping the little White kid to help me. I had dreams of becoming a poet, maybe even a rapper but all you saw was a thug, so that's what I became". A.D. was eloquent in his delivery as he told Talmadge how he had affected him. "I just bought that Escalade on Saturday and could not wait to see you on the road. Once we got onto King Drive I knew you would not just let me pass you without trying to race me. I never thought you would kill us".

Talmadge slowly got out of his chair and looked hard at A.D. "It was you in the black Escalade this morning? You were the fool who cut me off. I can't believe this. I tried to see who was driving but your tint was too dark. You killed me, you killed me!" Talmadge moved closer to A.D. as he continued to talk. A.D. stood fast watching as Talmadge moved his giant frame towards him. This time there would be no gun drawn, A.D. was defenseless.

Talmadge reached out and grabbed A.D. and embraced him. For the first time he was hugging a black man embracing him as a brother. "A.D. I am terribly sorry for what I have done to you. I was wrong and I know it is too late to make up for that now. Being here in this place I have been forced to examine myself and my life and the fact that you are the one who killed me in the end has brought me full circle". Talmadge looked at the thin man and smiled. "I understand the cycle now I do. I am ready to move on".

A.D. stepped back out of Talmadge's embrace and smiled. He only said three words "I forgive you", and then disappeared. Talmadge tried to grab him again, tried to feel the warm embrace of brotherhood but it eluded him. A.D. was gone. Only Talmadge and the thin man remained.

"You are not ready yet Talmadge, there is still one more person for you to meet." The thin man spoke softly as he rose from his seat and for the first time stepped into the light. Talmadge could finally see the thin mans face, but was truly unprepared for what he saw. He thought the thin man would be some white guy from his past, an old teacher, possibly even an old neighbor. He was neither. Talmadge had even wondered if the thin man would be another disfigured soul since his face had been hidden for so long, but it wasn't. Talmadge had even wondered if the face of the thin man would be that of Jesus

Christ himself, complete with long hair and a beard, but that was not the case either.

Talmadge recognized the thin man immediately. As soon as he stepped into the light there was no mistaking the thin man who stepped from the shadows, he was Coleman Talmadge Green. He was at least two hundred pounds thinner but he was still Talmadge. "Are you surprised?" the thin man asked as he walked closer to Talmadge who was now frozen in his tracks staring in disbelief.

"I don't know what to say - you are me - how is this possible?" asked Talmadge still in a daze. The other souls he had encountered were people he had actually done something to. He had not expected to ever see those people again but at least he understood their role as he waited in the anti-chamber. He had no idea of what to expect from himself.

"I am the soul that you should have had. I am the version of you that God had destined to do great things during his time on earth. Unfortunately you chose a different path. Each time you made a conscious decision to do that which was different from the path of universal truth and justice you got further and further away from bringing me into existence. You encountered many people on your journey through life. The things you did as a child were not counted against you. All children are born into sin it's the choices you made as an adult that have brought you face to face with who you should have become."

God and his fallen angel the devil are always trying to

test you. They both place people and obstacles in your life to see how you will respond. Each of the people you encountered represents one of the four virtues in life, faith, hope, charity, and love. Only a virtuous man can hope to enter the kingdom of heaven, and each person is given the opportunity to earn the virtues on his or her own merit. Prince and pauper, Black and White all are judged using the same scale.

Carlos Hosey tested your ability to provide charity. He only needed a little personal assistance from you, but you refused to give that which we all have the ability to give a piece of yourself. Glenda Jean Spencer the woman you simply referred to as the cleaning lady tested your ability to inspire hope in your fellow man. She admired you from your first day in the office. She could see her grandson in you. She had hoped that he would become successful like you but when you were in trouble she hoped that you would overcome your demons and believed in you enough to put her self on the line for you. Once again you demonstrated that you had no hope for your fellow human beings. You placed a value on her based on her occupation not on her humanity."

"Adrian "A.D". Williams tested your sense of faith. He too admired you and needed you to believe in his ability to overcome his environment. All he needed was for you to see beyond his circumstances and support him as he attempted to do that which was right. By forcing him to leave the community center you destroyed his faith in the system. He could see no other way except the streets and a life of crime to gain all of the material things he saw you with. He assumed based on your treatment of him that no one would ever see him for the talented writer that he was. You destroyed his faith in himself and his abilities."

"Finally, there was Teresa Sapphire, who tested you on the virtue of love. At first thought one might believe that your wife should have been the one to test you on the virtue of love, but that was not the case. Teresa was someone who trusted you while you were already involved with others. Her interest in you although based in part on all of the lies you told represented a sincere form of love. Through her you could have truly found a friend to love instead you tried to find a concubine, another plaything. Your inability to understand love in its purest form from one friend to another is probably the worst decision you could have made among your transgressions. It is also the one, which ended in the most painful death. Teresa died embarrassed, slow and almost alone. Your love for one you called a brother was also tested. You voluntarily swore an oath before God when you were married as well as when you joined your fraternity, in dealing with one woman you broke both". The thin mans summary was by far the most devastating testimony Talmadge had heard thus far. There was no escaping the reality, the honesty of it all. Talmadge had been tested and had failed, and now was wondering what the consequences of his failure would be. A simple "now what?" was all he could fix his lips to say.

"I wish I could say things are going to work out for you Talmadge, that somehow things were going to get better for you. I told you earlier that you had to face five black people in order to move on. I have explained how your interaction with four of them has resulted in you being placed here for judgment. I have not explained the fifth black person to you". There was an ominous tone in the thin mans voice as he spoke to Talmadge. It was not harsh, nor cold, but it did reflect a certain level of approaching finality."

"The soul you see before you now is indeed your soul. I, in my thin form represent all that you should and would have become had you just done what was right and passed the test. The extra weight you carry was given to you as a warning sign that you were fast approaching a dangerous place in your life. Every act of treachery and deceit gained you more poundage. Even your addiction to alcohol was an attempt from higher powers to get you to seek help and change your life. Did you ever notice how much more you drank after your encounters with each of these people in real life? By the time of Teresa's death you were a serious alcoholic, trying to drink away your fears about H.I.V. and A.I.D.S. If only you had turned to God things would have been so different."

"In this life everyone is given a chance to meet five black people and be judged on their interaction with them. The judgment does not happen when you arrive here at the anti-chamber it happens on Earth when you meet the people in real life. One never knows if the black person on the elevator that you never speak to is a test. One never knows if the black person who collects your trash is the test. The same with the black professor who's class you refuse to take, or doctor you refuse to be examined by, you never know when you are being tested. Talmadge your fifth person is yourself in part because of your hatred of black people. Despite the fact that you yourself are a black man you have found every reason to distrust other black men, and disrespect other black people in general. Everything you did to the blacks that were placed in your life demonstrates your own self-hatred. If you had only embraced your heritage you would have been so much more successful. Carlos would have become your business partner, and the two of you would have had a hugely successful accounting firm. Glenda Jean Spencer would have met you when she retired, your accounting firm would have managed her pension and retirement funds which would have been quite substantial given her years of employment with Arthur Anderson. She lost all of that when she was fired. Her grandson Cedric would have completed an internship in your office, and eventually would have worked for you upon his graduation from Northwestern. Adrian Williams would have become an extremely successful author and professor of black literature. He would have used your firm for his accounting needs and been instrumental in connecting you to the international African business community. Teresa would have proven to be one of your dearest friends and confidants.

She and Anthony would have been married and shared many happy moments vacationing and visiting with you and your family."

Talmadge was on both knees looking up as images of everything that the thin man said were flashing before him. He cried out loud as the visuals became too much for him to bear. The card table disappeared first, and then the hanging light fixture vanished. One by one each of the visuals as described by the thin man began to disappear until all that remained was Talmadge and the thin man.

"It is now time for you to move on Talmadge," said the thin man. Before Talmadge could ask him where he was going, the thin man disappeared. Talmadge looked around to see if anyone else was going to appear. That's when he felt the heat. It was an unbearable type of heat unlike any he had ever felt before. The flames were all around him. As he looked in the distance he could see rooms all around him. Each room contained one person and outside of every room stood five black people all waiting patiently for their turn to enter one of the rooms. He recognized some of the people but most he did not know. The one thing he was sure of is that each of them would have to relive the mistakes of their lives just as he had. Suddenly, a door in his room opened and in walked the disfigured soul of Carlos Hosey. Talmadge finally understood. It was a circle, he had created these unfortunate souls and now he was going to spend an eternity with each of them, reliving the painful manner in which he had impacted their lives.

"Hi Cheese, old boy - you looked surprised to see me" Carlos began. Talmadge wept aloud and screamed "Noooo!" as the flames engulfed him and the four other souls stood patiently outside his room waiting their turn to speak with him again.

The End

NOTES

Discussion Guide / Human Potential

1) Do you have five black people in your past that you would be afraid to be judged based on your past interactions with them?

2) Based on how you have lived your life thus far which of the characters in the book would you see yourself reflected in? Why?

3) Discuss a time in your life where you found it difficult to face yourself as a result of your own actions or due to another's actions toward you?

4) What did you do in order to resolve the internal conflict caused by your answer to question number three?

5) Do you know people who use food, drugs, and/or alcohol as a means of not dealing with personal issues in their own lives? How does that relate to the characters in the book?

6) Which of the characters in the book were equally as responsible for their fate as Talmadge was? Why do you believe that?

7) Which of the characters had little to no responsibility for their fate and were truly victimized by Talmadge?

8) What do you believe is the reason that Talmadge turned out to be the way that he is?

9) Is it harder to forgive or be forgiven?

10) What lengths are you willing to go through in order to forgive versus what lengths you go through to stay mad or seek revenge?

NOTES

Discussion Guide / Christiantity

1) How are the seven deadly sins represented in the story?

2) Can you think of a Bible verse that might have helped each of the characters work through each of their particular situation?

3) Which of the "Ten Commandments" (from Christianity) were broken by characters in the story?

4) What role do you think faith played in the lives of the characters of the book? Use examples form the book to support your opinion.

5) Should any of the characters in the book get into heaven? Why or why not?

6) Can you think of a story from the Bible that talks about forgiveness that would be comparable to the situations any of the characters in the book found themselves in?

7) "Heaven" is mentioned in the title of the book, why do you believe "Hell" is not prominently featured in the book?

8) Using examples from the book discuss how Talmadge was able to tempt others into disobeying the laws of God?

9) Select one character in the book and describe a prayer you would offer for them had they come to you for guidance, or support for what they were experiencing?

10) Which of the acts that Talmadge committed would be hard for you to forgive if he had committed those same transgressions against you?

NOTES

Personal Reflection Discussion Guide

1) Do you have five black people in your past that you would be afraid to be judged based on your past interactions with them?

2) Based on how you have lived your life thus far which of the characters in the book would you see yourself reflected in? Why?

3) Discuss a time in your life where you found it difficult to face yourself as a result of your own actions or due to another's actions toward you?

4) What did you do in order to resolve the internal conflict caused by your answer to question number three?

5) Do you know people who use food, drugs, and/or alcohol as a means of not dealing with personal issues in their own lives? How does that relate to the characters in the book?

6) Which of the characters in the book were equally as responsible for their fate as Talmadge was? Why do you believe that?

7) Which of the characters had little to no responsibility for their fate and were truly victimized by Talmadge?

8) What do you believe is the reason that Talmadge turned out to be the way that he is?

9) Is it harder to forgive or be forgiven?

10) What lengths are you willing to go through in order to forgive versus what lengths you go through to stay mad or seek revenge?

NOTES

Resources & Information

February 7 is National Black HIV/AIDS Awareness Day.

March 10 is National Women and Girls HIV/AIDS Awareness Day.

March 20 is National Native (American Indian, Alaska Native, and Native Hawaiian) HIV/AIDS Awareness Day.

May 19 is National Asian and Pacific Islander (API) HIV/AIDS Awareness Day.

June 8 is Caribbean American HIV/AIDS Awareness Day.

June 27 is National HIV Testing Day.

October 15 is National Latino AIDS Awareness Day.

December 1st. is World AIDS Day.

Center For Disease Control HIV Fact Sheet & Info:
  http://www.cdc.gov/hiv/resources/factsheets/

Alcoholics Anonymous:
  http://www.aa.org

Sexual Addiction Self Test & Information:
  http://www.sexhelp.com/sast.cfm

NOTES

Nurturing Action Steps

1) Practice forgiveness, begin by forgiving yourself.

2) Live each day so that your actions assist others in maximizing their potential.

3) Spend time reflecting on your words and actions as well as on planning your future words and actions.

4) Be intentional in all of your actions, don't allow your past or present situation to limit your future.

5) Don't look to drugs, alcohol, or other vices to make you feel special. You are special!

6) Know your personal worth no one can make you feel insignificant without your permission.

7) Invest your money and your time in your future.

8) Find and pursue your passion.

9) Look for, find, and share a reason to smile each and every single day/

10) Tell someone "thank you", before you have to say, "I'm sorry..."

NOTES

HIV/AIDS Action Steps

1) Get tested for HIV.
2) Practice safe methods to prevent HIV.
3) Decide not to engage in high-risk behaviors.
4) Talk about HIV prevention with family, friends and colleagues.
5) Provide support to people living with HIV/AIDS.
6) Get involved with or host an event for National HIV/AIDS Awareness Day in your community.

About The Author

Bryant K. Smith is a man with a vision. He is an expert in identifying, cultivating, and maximizing human potential. His work often makes good people great and great people memorable. For the past two decades Bryant has been at the forefront of assisting business, athletic, and educational institutions train, inspire, and develop their employees, athletes, and students into potentially world altering people. Driven, outspoken, and passionate Bryant's enthusiasm for helping others combined with his exceptional communication skills have taken him from the public schools of his hometown Chicago into some of the nations leading, business, and educational institutions.

Known for his ability to "meet his clients where they are and guide them to where they need to be" Bryant uses his life motto "difficult does not equal impossible" as a reminder that success is only one more attempt away. Bryant K. Smith is the President and Founder of Smith Consulting And Networking a premiere comprehensive consulting, training, and development firm. Bryant is also the author of a social commentary on race relations in the United States entitled "Black Not Blind", and 'M.A.N.-U.P. How To Coach A male Into Manhood" Bryant invites you all to M.A.N.-U.P. "Master And Nurture (your) Unlimited Potential!" More info about Bryant and his work can be found at **www.Smithcan.com**

Thank You

Dear Reader, thank you for taking time to share with me the joy of reading. It is my hope that you found my work enjoyable and will suggest my book to your friends, family, and colleagues who also enjoy reading. I also encourage you to examine some of the engaging, and life changing empowerment and development workshops that I conduct for businesses, schools, and communities by examining my website at **www.Smithcan.com**.